Why Do We Age

By
Hilton Hotema

ISBN: 978-1-63923-470-7

Printed: August 2022

Cover Art By: Amit Paul

Published and Distributed By:
Lushena Books
607 Country Club Drive, Unit E
Bensenville, IL 60106
www.lushenabooksinc.com/books

ISBN: 978-1-63923-470-7

WHY DO WE AGE

By

Hilton Hotema

NOTICE

The statements contained in this work are recitals of scientific findings, known facts of biology and physiology, and references to ancient writings, as they are found extant. No claim is made as to what the methods cited may do for one in any given case, and the publisher assumes no obligation for the options advanced and the conclusions expressed.

"Honest investigations and unprejudiced criticism lead to Light and Liberty, whereas all forms of censorship and suppression lead to darkness and enslavement."

"You think the Dark Ages are gone because you are asleep. AWAKE! Your boasted liberty and enlightenment are largely imaginary. You cannot miss what you never had."

WHY DO WE AGE

Also by Hilton Hotema:

The Great Law

The Genesis of Christianity

Mystery of Man

The Mysterious Sphinx

The Great Red Dragon

Hilton Hotema

Contents

WHY DO WE AGE

BLOOD OF LIFE

"Beware when the great God lets loose a thinker on this planet. Then all things are at risk. It is as when a conflagration has broken out in great city, and no man knows what is safe, or where it will end. There is not a piece of science, but its flank may be turned tomorrow. There is not any literary reputation, not the so-called eternal names of fame, that may not be reviled and condemned. The very hopes of man, the thoughts of his heart, the religion of nations, the manners and morals of mankind, are all at the mercy of a new generalization. Generalization is always a new influx of the Divinity into the mind. Hence the thrill that attends it." (Emerson's Essays)

"For the Life of the Flesh is IN the blood" (Lev. 17:11).

The Breath, not the Blood, maintains and sustains the body. When you stop breathing you stop living. Try it sometime and see. Make that simple experiment yourself.

The function of respiration is the secret of living. To maintain and sustain the living organism demands:
1. constant breathing,
2. constant absorption by the blood of gases in the lungs, and
3. constant elimination of the toxic substances produced in the body.

The air in the lungs is a composition of invisible gaseous substance. The blood is a mass of corpuscles floating in the fluid plasma. An analysis shows that the blood contains oxygen, carbon dioxide and nitrogen -- gases of the air. There may be others that are as yet undiscovered. The corpuscles are the carriers, and the plasma is the fluid in which they float.

The blood is the medium by which these gases are conveyed from the lungs to the billions of body cells, and also by which the poisonous substances produced by disintegration are carried off and disposed of thru the channels of elimination.

The blood per se nourishes nothing. It is not, technically speaking, a stream of nutrition, but a system of transportation, as a railroad that carries farm products to the cities for use as food, and carries off the garbage.

The primary purpose of eating and drinking is not to supply the blood with nourishment for the body but to furnish materials to maintain this unique transportation system, that it may always be competent to carry to the body cells, the gases of the air that are the actual builders and sustainers of the body.

The body, from its embryonic stage till birth and death, is maintained by a process of cell division, not by food. When the cell is ready to divide, it shakes violently and tosses its contents in all directions. The two parts into which the cell divides, withdraw from each other and become two new, individualized cells of the body.

WHY DO WE AGE

In no wise does the cell resemble the favorite abstraction of the chemist-- "a drop of gelatin surrounded by a semi-permeable membrane"; and protoplasm, a concept with no objective meaning, is not as claimed by biologists, found in either the nucleus or in the structure of the cell.

The structural complexity of the living cell is not only disconcerting to biologists, but its chemical constitution is still more intricate. The simplicity attributed by the chemist to the cell's constituent nucleoproteins is an illusion.

Carrel sums up this scientific speculation by declaring that "our ignorance (of the human body) is profound" (P. 4). In plainer words, what is accepted as scientific knowledge of the body's constitution and function is common nonsense.

When so-called medical science knows so little about the body cells, it knows just as little about the body. For the body is but a mass of millions of cells. The cells are actually tiny suns and stars, similarly constituted and composed of the same cosmic substance.

Man does not eat and drink to nourish the atoms in the cells of which the body is built. These atoms are eternal and self-sustaining.

Man is urged to eat freely to nourish his body, to build up his strength and resist disease. It is claimed that the body is animated, vitalized, nourished and sustained by food by means of a direct chemical process. Yet the process cannot be analyzed or explained in an intelligent and logical manner, for that alleged process is purely imaginary.

The total quantity of air that passes into and out of the lungs of an adult, at rest, in 24 hours, is about 686,000 cubic inches. But in the case of a hard-working man the average amount in the same time is 1,568,390 cubic inches—an increase of 882,390 cubic inches, or more than double the amount at rest (P.283).

Why the great increase? To supply the amount of gases needed for new cells and to replace the cells consumed by the increased activity.

This is more proof that the cells are built of the gases of the air, not of food, and these cells build all organs and tissues of the body.

In his "Believe It or Not," Ripley said that Gilman Lowe, weight lifter and health director, after fasting for three weeks, mounted a scale adjusted to 1,000 pounds net. The scale was equipped with a steel platform, against which Lowe braced his back. He braced and lifted 1,006 times in succession, until the scale each time registered half a ton – a total of 1,006,000 pounds, in 34 minutes and 35 seconds. (New York, 1903)

Lowe did that after eating nothing for three weeks. Every test of strength and endurance shows that man's strength and vitality depend on the gases of the air, not on food. But

8

this is usually overlooked. Food does not nourish the body. Food does not and cannot produce the body; nor can food sustain what it cannot produce.

The body is built of cells, not of food; and the cells are not built of food but of atoms. Cells disintegrate and must be replaced; but food does not supply the replacement of cells.

Dr. J.C. Dalton, in his work on Physiology, wrote; "A continuous change goes on in the substance of the body and its organs, by which their materials are constantly decomposed and constantly renewed. Throughout the whole frame, vital force is incessantly engaged in taking apart the tissues of which the body is composed, and in building them over again of new, fresh materials, so that the tissues of the body are accordingly always renewed and always ready to perform their allotted work."

Renewing the body tissues is most certainly not nourishing them. The process of so-called nutrition cannot be explained because there is no such process.

The body tissues are renewed, not nourished. Cell by cell the body disintegrates, and cell by cell the body re-integrates.

The body is the product of electrons, atoms, and molecules, which build the cells which build the body. These "building blocks" as Millikan terms them, are not the product of food.

The vital processes of the body are beyond the ken of man. They cannot be traced to their ultimate origin, except in the Mind. Attempts to do so lead to a point of irresistible opposition to further analysis by physical science.

We trace back through the cells, molecules and atoms to the electrons, which are found to be whirling centers of force in the ether. In the Mind we may reverse the process and visualize those whirling centers of force, condensing into visible elements, forms, and entities, by a natural process, resulting from a retardation of the vibrations.

It is common knowledge that astral substance thus condenses to form water, ice and other visible compounds. It should be as easy to understand that invisible, astral substance condenses, under the same law, to form cells, flesh, bone and the body.

The body appears as a material form. So does a block of ice. But that material is condensed astral substance, just as water is condensed gases of the air.

The body is composed and constituted of astral substance, and produced and sustained by a astral process of liquification, condensation, and transformation. It is not built of food by a physico-chemical process.

The absolute and uninterrupted persistence of the function of respiration is the leading wonder of the living body.

WHY DO WE AGE

When the new born babe takes its first breath, it begins the breathing that will never cases except in death. It's cessation for only a few minutes means death.

Man can go for days without drinking and for weeks without eating, but breathing under all circumstances must be continuous or death ensues.

Body cells are built of liquefied gases and nothing else. These gases are a combination of atoms which are a combination of electrons.

Food and drink do not directly enter into the building process, except as they furnish gaseous elements that enter into cell construction.

Cell disintegration produces nothing but liquefied gases. These gases are a combination of atoms and nothing else. These gaseous products are eliminated from the body through the lungs, the bladder and the skin.

The body cells are actually tiny stars and suns. The chemical elements of which all bodies are built, from star above to man below, are the same. These elements never change nor lose their cosmic identity. They enter into the composition of everything, from star to man, and are always governed by the same law.

The skin is impervious, to a certain extent, to these invisible gaseous, atomic elements. But the lining membrane of the lungs and intestines is so constituted as to permit these elements to pass through and enter the blood.

These atomic elements retain their cosmic identity in man's body just as they do in all other bodies, from the atom in the human cell to the atom in the giant star. They do not depend on food and drink in the star nor in the body.

Atoms are composed of electrons, and Dr. Robert Milliken, Dean of California Institute of Technology, terms electrons "the building blocks of the Universe." They do not depend on food and drink.

If any naturopath, dietician or nutritional expert, or food scientist desires to dispute these statements, let him first explain the following:--
Patients said by doctors to be suffering from malnutrition, or from any deficiency disorder, or from so-called mineral starvation, or lack of vitamins, invariably recover from such conditions under a fast, taking into their stomach nothing but water to maintain the transportation system.

That is not a theory but a fact of common knowledge among doctors who practice the fasting of patients. This evidence shows that improper food or lack of proper food is not the direct cause of the condition.

The direct cause of the condition is the interference of the food the patient eats with the blood's ability to absorb from the lungs the amount of gaseous substance required by the body cells.

When this interference is removed by fasting, and the patient is supplied with fresh air and good water, the blood is soon able to resume and perform its function efficiently.

There is an additional direct cause that arises from breathing the polluted air of civilization.

One of America's leading physicians declared that he believed 98 percent of all disorders are due to the presence of too much carbon acid gas in the body.

Dr. L. Burns examined blood specimens of 25,000 persons, in his study of the effects of carbon monoxide gases on the blood. He found that--"Carbon Monoxide gas seeps into the blood through the lungs and mixes with the hemoglobin to such an extent that the blood cannot perform its function of carrying oxygen to the body cells."

The function of the hemoglobin is to carry oxygen to the cells. When charged with oxygen it is called oxyhemoglobin.

It may seem strange that the hemoglobin has a special affinity for carbon monoxide gas of approximately 300 times greater than for oxygen.

The amount of carbon monoxide taken up by the hemoglobin is equal to the amount of oxygen displaced. While carbon monoxide gas readily displaces oxygen, the reverse is not the case; and upon this property depends the very dangerous effect of carbon monoxide poisoning.

The condition is less serious in country homes, except in winter when cold weather is making it necessary to close doors and windows for comfort. Then all the people in rural regions suffer more or less from varying degree of carbon monoxide and carbonic acid poisoning.

Carbon monoxide and carbonic acid poisoning are the chief cause of colds and all ailments of the air organs, and of those dull, deep-seated aches and pains (rheumatism) which appear in later life.

As the oxygen level of the blood falls below normal by reason of being displaced by the deadly carbon monoxide and carbon dioxide gases, there is not sufficient oxygen in the blood to supply the placement cells.

The fact that man must breathe without a minute's cessation from birth to death stamps this function as one of the paramount importance. Just as important is the kind and condition of the air one breathes.

Why do people die of starvation when deprived of food? That is a good question and is fully considered in a later lesson.

BREATH OF DEATH

"Without the meeting of the air and the blood, the life of the Temple would end at once. Hence it has been so arranged that the air and the blood cannot fail to meet. When the river of life, dark with poisons, flows from the right ventricle of the heart through the pulmonary artery into the lungs, it always finds the air waiting in the tiny breathing rooms." – F.M. Rossiter, B.S., M.D., Story of the Human Body.

What kind of air does the blood find waiting in the tiny breathing rooms? Man knows he must breathe to live, but he thinks the KIND of air he inhales is not important.

You have heard of the Breath of Life (Gen. 2:7), but you may never have heard of the Breath of Death.

The function of Respiration is a dual process of Life and Death. Inspiration, to live carries Life into the body, and expiration, to die, carries Death out of the body.

Like all other processes, this one produces results according to the conditions supplied. Under the same condition the same result is obtained. Under change of condition, it is evident there must be a correspondent change of result.

Man is vigorous when he supplies the conditions that produce it. He dies suddenly or by slow degrees as he supplies conditions that produce these results.

Inspiration may carry either Life or Death into the body, depending on the kind of air one breathes: Inspiration carries Death into the body if the air inhaled is vitiated. When the inhaled air contains enough poison, death comes quickly.

A thousand persons died in less than two minutes when they inhaled the poisoned air in Hitler's gas chambers in World War II. Millions of people, all over the world, are constantly dying by slow degrees from effects of the vitiated air they breathe.

The Breath of Life is fresh, clean, outside air, in which birds and beasts live in health and vigor.

The Breath of Death is the foul, stagnant, polluted, poisoned air of civilization, in which live civilized man, the sick and ailing, the feeble and decrepit.

In this lesson we shall observe only the subject of air pollution by poisons emanating from man's body. An adult poisons nearly a barrel full of air at each exhalation. The poisonous gases are brought by the blood to the lungs and eliminated. They consist of carbonic, lactic, hydrochloric, phosphoric and other acids, and are the products of cell disintegration incessantly occurring in the body.

Cell disintegration liberates into a fluid medium large quantities of these poisonous acids. A cell must receive a volume of fluid equal to 2,000 times its own volume, and a volume of gaseous substance at least 20,000 times its own volume, in order not to be seriously poisoned within a few days by the disintegrated products of the cells.

That explains the basic reason:
1. Why man should drink more than he eats,
2. Why the body needs fluid more than it needs food,
3. Why man must incessantly inhale the gaseous substance called air, or quickly die.

He does die by degrees from inhaling polluted air that fills his body with many ailments, the symptoms of which are given names and foolishly termed "disease".

It is the marvelous perfection of the Transportation System that enables the body to live in a volume of blood hardly equal to one-tenth of its own weight. The speed of the circulation is sufficiently swift to prevent the composition of the blood, under normal conditions, from being modified by the products of cell disintegration. But that composition is seriously modified by the polluted air that man inhales.

During its passage through the lungs, the blood disposes of carbonic acid chiefly. This is the most common of deadly gases in the air of homes and hospitals, and is seldom seriously considered.

This gas has the distinction of killing quicker than any other poison. Quicker than the venom of a rattler.

That is the dangerous character of the gas exhaled in the Breath of Death. It saturates the air of homes in winter when cold weather makes adequate ventilation impracticable. It is breathed over and over again, poisoning the body through and through, and causing the members of the home to suffer from many ailments, for which poisonous remedies are taken while fresh air is never suggested for relief. In fact, fresh air is considered so dangerous that windows are closed to keep out the terrible draft. Yet, in these drafts the birds and beasts live in health.

Carbon dioxide is more dangerous because its presence cannot be detected by the five senses. It is colourless, odourless and tasteless. Combined with hydrogen gas, it forms the common firecamp that sends many a brave miner to his death, and is the most feared of all underground enemies.

The atmosphere contains about one part of carbon dioxide to 2,500 parts of air a very small proportion. But this gas has a tendency to sink to the ground and in low places.

When there are three parts of carbon dioxide in 100 parts of the air, a drowsy feeling is felt, and this can be relived only by fresh air. When present in the proportion of four parts in 100 parts of the air, it is a fatal poison. When present in larger proportion, it is quick in effect and leaves no hope for aid or recovery.

As this gas sinks to the ground, it is sometimes found in large quantities in wells sunk in marshes and low lands. One author says...

"A man went into a well in sight of his family. He failed to respond to a call, and they found him dead. His demise was instantaneous. Thousands of such cases have occurred and are occurring."

"The gas in sewers is also due to the presence of this same poison. A man went through a manhole into a sewer only a few feet below the ground level. Not returning in due time, a companion went down after him. As he failed to return, a third started to enter, but was stopped by the fourth. The first two were found dead, having died in a second of time by inhaling carbon-dioxide."

All the blood passes through the lungs many times every hour, eliminating carbon-dioxide gas and absorbing in the lungs, the oxygen needed by the cells, and without which death would quickly occur.

When not promptly eliminated from the body, carbon-dioxide leaves a trail of damage in its course through the organism. It affects every cell, and in the cells is where the deterioration begins which ends only at the grave.

Carbon-dioxide is present in all charged drinks, in all soda waters, all beverages of the soda kind, in beer and fermented liquids, in cake, bread, baking powder cookery, self rising flour products, yeast bread, and in all fermenting products.

The air exhaled from the lungs at each **breath** contains a large proportion of **carbon**-dioxide and a minute amount of organic matter.

If this **exhaled** air be breathed again and again, as it is in homes and hospitals, the proportion of carbon-dioxide and organic matter in it will incessantly increase until it becomes more dangerous to breathe.

That is the main reason why many patients develop pneumonia in hospitals, especially after operations. Their bodies are poisoned through and through with the anesthetics administered to paralyze the nerve system sufficiently that the body is insensible to pain, and, in addition to this poisoning, comes the carbon-dioxide in the air the victim breathes. Lucky is he who gets out of it alive.

The first symptoms of carbon-dioxide poisoning are sensation of uneasiness, drowsiness, sneezing, languor, headache, sense of oppression, coughs and colds.

The secret that deceives is the fact that the body, after a time, adjusts or adapts itself to a very vitiated atmosphere, and a person soon becomes breathing without sensible discomfort, an atmosphere which, when he first enters it, seems intolerable.

This adaptation is termed "immunity". According to this theory, man becomes immune to a condition or poison if it does not kill him on the spot.

Such adaptation can occur only at the expense of a general depression of all the vital functions, which must be injurious if long continued or often repeated. It is in this condition that people die by inches while being treated for some "mysterious diseases."

Spencer said that eternal physical existence depends upon perfect correspondence between the organism and its environment, and that man dies because changes occur in the environment which the organism has not adapted changes to meet.

Man was never made to live in an atmosphere so foul, that each breath puts more poisons in his body. Breathing should be a process of purification instead of a process of poisoning.

Every sneeze, every cough, every cold, every headache-- These are the first warnings that man is breathing polluted air. He fails to heed these signals. He does not understand them, and takes poisonous remedies to depress further the vital functions and kill the symptoms, while he continues to breathe the same vitiated air.

The body is so perfectly equipped with power of adaptation that it will adjust itself in time to tolerate an atmosphere so poisonous that it would kill a vital, healthy man in a few moments if he suddenly walked into it.

This wonderful, mysterious, little-understood power of adaptation of the living organism to its environment is well illustrated by an experience of Claude Bernard.

For instance, if a bird be placed in under a bell-glass of such size that the bird will live for three hours, and is removed at the end of the second hour when it could have survived another hour, and a fresh healthy bird be put in its place, the latter will die immediately.

That is a demonstration of the body's power of adaptation. That is the power of the body that enables poisoned, civilized man to drag out a miserable existence of 50 or 60 years in an environment that would quickly kill a vigorous, healthy, wild Indian, brought in from the pure air of the woods and hills and thrust into that environment.

Building up the body's power to resist disease is getting off on the wrong track- the more this is done the more scientific the masses think it is. Darkness is highly useful to hide ignorance and error.

Due to the body's power of adaptation, people can live constantly in polluted air and, on the surface, suffer nothing more than coughs, colds, hay fever, sore throat, and other mild ailments of the air organs. Yet they are dying by inches from the effects of that air and know it not.

WHY DO WE AGE

You are learning how your spiritual Chambers are ruined while you are still a child.

Sixty to 80 times per minute the purple, poisonous river of life flows from the heart to the lungs, into the millions of tiny air-cells that form a vast network of meeting places for the blood and the air. The walls of the blood capillaries in the air cells are thinner than the walls of soap bubbles. Only the slightest film separates the air and the blood in the lungs.

Air once breathed is unfit to breathe again. It is saturated with poisons and if inhaled again, it poisons all the cells of the body. Every person in a room requires 3,000 cubic feet of air an hour.

After an apartment has been occupied sixty minutes, the air in it should be as pure as it was at first. Ventilation that is less than this is insufficient. For every impurity in the air must be inhaled by the occupants, and these impurities poison their bodies to a corresponding degree.

There must always be perfect correspondence between the organism and its environment. When the babe is born with perfect body, that body does not correspond with the polluted environment of civilization.

Since the state of the environment cannot be improved and made to correspond to the high state of the body, then the condition of the body must be impaired to bring it down to harmonize with its environment.

The discord is removed by a series of ailments, stupidly termed "children's diseases" – as is the statement that children MUST have them. And they must have them or migrate to a better environment. For the physical state of the body must correspond with the polluted state of its environment. So the discord must be removed, and is removed by a process of degeneration.

This philosophy sounds strange to you only because your mind is controlled by the social pattern.

We observe that the function of breathing is a dual process of living and dying, extending from birth to death.

Man's health continues good so long as health rules are observed and this double process remains in perfect equilibrium. Physical decline begins when the balance is distributed or destroyed, regardless of what one eats or drinks.

The physical condition of the body can never be better than the condition of the air one breathes. Let no dietician deceive you on that point.

At each inspiration, the Breath of Life enters the body to build new cells; and at each expiration the Breath of Death leaves the body with its load of dead cells.

WHY DO WE AGE

The Breath of Life and the Breath of Death are literal and not allegorical terms. The breath of Death is composed of dead cells leaving the body in gaseous form. The expired air should not be breathed again. If it is, the dead cell gases enter the body, not to vitalize it but to vitiate it.

If the inspired air is contaminated with the deadly gases of disintegrated cells, the process of cell-replacement becomes that of cell-poisoning. Then the Breath of Life actually and literally becomes the Breath of Death.

Here also the Ancient Masters showed their superior wisdom. They termed the expired air the Black Breath of Death, and taught their disciples to visualize it as black as soot – a stream in which all the evils of mind and body, all weaknesses and infirmities, flow from the organism.

Doors and windows of homes should always be open, and bed clothes and pillows should be daily aired. How can that be done in winter in the land of ice and snow?

Science above that man, by nature, is a tropical being, and not adapted to the cold zone. Man is made to live in the open air and sunshine, with the birds and beasts. This is the law. If violated, the penalty must be paid.

BREATHING IS LIVING

When you stop breathing you stop living, no matter how good may be your heart. Most cases of death from heart failure are due to polluted air and not to the condition of the heart.

The network of blood capillaries in the lungs are distributed everywhere in the minute spaces between the billions of air vesicles, and envelope their walls within a vascular screen.

The blood flows through the lungs in billions of small currents, almost in direct contact with the air in the lungs. In fact, it is as though the River of Living Water were sprayed thru the Breath of Life in an exceedingly fine shower of Red Mist, so that every particle of Blood and every particle of Air in the lungs are brought together in the closest possible proximity.

1. The blood, from all parts of the body, goes to the heart and then goes directly to the lungs thru the right and left pulmonary arteries, the only arteries in the blood that carry venous blood.
2. This blood flowing from the heart to the lungs, is of a dark blue color, approaching to black.
3. This is venous blood, and is saturated through and through with all the filth, waste, pollution, and poison collected from the cells, tissues, organs, glands, and blood vessels of the body.
4. The blood is now a filty stream of poison in the broadest sense of the word, flowing to the heart thru the great veins from all over the body, to be sent on to the lungs

for renovation and purification. Unless the process of purification occurs quickly, without undue interferences, death soon ensues.

5. As the purging process occurs in the lungs, a marvelous change occurs in the colur of the blood. At the very instance that the poisonous blood passes into the air-cells, a lightning exchange takes place between the blood and the air, in which the color of the blood becomes a brilliant scarlet, due to the passage of the poison in the blood into the air-cells of the lungs, and eliminated and expelled as invisible vapor in the process of exhalation.

6. This process of Blood purification, by which the blood exchanges its poisonous gases for the air gases in the lungs, occurs approximately 2,880 times every 24 hours, in which time approximately 125 barrels of blood are purified in the lungs.

Now you see why it is so important to know the condition of the air you breathe. If you live in the polluted air of the city, that is the kind of air gases the blood must take up in the lungs, and that is the kind of air in which city dwellers live.

That fact shows that Dr. Parkes was right in the 19th century, when he declared that all the causes of disease, breathing vitiated air is the chief.

And those diseases medical art attempts to "cure" by the use of other poisons in the form of drugs and nostrums, vaccines and serums, while paying little or no attention to the kind of air people breathe.

BLOOD POISON

In the polluted environment of civilization, where a breath of really pure air is not to be found, as the poisoned blood flows to the lungs for purification, there is simply an exchange of poisonous gases.

This is a condition of Blood Poison, and this condition must occur before you can have the slightest ailment, -- even the common cold. In 1923 we wrote a booklet on the subject, in which we said:

1. Astral Radiation is the creative force. In health it works smoothly and silently. When its function is obstructed, it struggles to save its Temple by removing the obstructing object or condition.
   The surface symptoms of this internal struggle is what medical art calls "disease", giving it names according to the situs of the symptoms, and then treats the condition as though it were a destructive process. There is no such thing as disease per se.
2. The continuous and harmonious existence of the organism depends upon strict compliance with the Law of Life, written in every fiber of its structure.
3. The living organism, as a machine, is perfect, and needs nothing but the greatest freedom to perform its work in harmony with the law.

4. The only healing power on earth is within the body itself, and can be aided by nothing but the body-sustaining agencies of the universe.

5. No force, no machine, no substance or thing, no drugs, nostrums, vaccine or serums, are able to save the body or serve its healing power.

6. The condition of the body depends upon the condition of the blood, and the condition of the blood depends upon the air we breathe, the fluid we drink, and the food we eat.

7. Insofar as the blood remains active and normal, and to that degree only, will and must all organs and parts of the body remain in health.

8. In direct ratio as the blood becomes as stagnant, impure, and abnormal will and must all organs and parts of the body decline from health. This is not disease but degeneration, with only death as the end of it all.

9. As the condition of the blood is, so must the condition of the body be. For as the condition of the body depends upon the condition of the blood, it follows that good health or bad health depends upon and rises from the blood.

10. The River of Living Water that turns the Wheels of Life, is not only the health-building and life-sustaining agency, but is also the destructive power. Therefore, the doctor worthy of the title is he who understands the Principles of Biology and Physiology, and he takes the following position:

A. The condition of the body depends upon the condition of the blood.
B. The normal flow of normal blood builds good health.
C. Retarded circulation and polluted blood build bad health.
D. Purification of the blood and acceleration of its circulation is scientific and effective treatment of bad health.
E. The means to accomplish this purpose are supplied only by the body. Only the body makes blood and purifies it. Nothing else can do the work. The greatest chemist cannot make a drop of blood; nor can he make any substance or concoction to improve blood.
F. The source of supply determines the method of procedure.
G. The procedure must be natural and according to cosmic law. Then the results are and must be favorable and permanent.

Our language is simple and our explanations are clear because we realize that technical statements cannot be properly comprehended by 13-year-old Minds, not intelligently understood by more than 14% of the masses, who are as a rule poisoned thru and thru with polluted air.

These figures on Mind and Brain capacity are the scientific findings of psychologists.

If the best doctor on earth should study the subject of good and bad health for a century, he would come back to what has been said here about the blood, and positively declare, There is it; it is all there.

This simple, understandable philosophy concerning the River of Life, gives the reader a full and complete answer to that puzzling question, What is disease?

REJUVENATION

Harvey's discovery of the circulation of the blood revealed that the River of Living Water is the real Fountain of Youth. By its action, every cell of the body, every minute of time, is cleansed of the waste products of its work kept in proper condition for its work.

This newly discovered secret medical art knows not how to use. The details of the procedure are unknown to medical doctors. Medical text books contain nothing on the subject. For the Holy Medical Authorities who wrote the books knew nothing of the secret. So the puzzled doctors of the rank and file slyly ask one another: "Why does the body seem to grow old and die? How can it wear out? Why does it not go on forever?"

When the great Metchnikoff answered these questions, he met the same jeers from his medical brethren that greeted Harvey when he announced his discovery of the circulation of the blood.

31

After years of investigation, Metchnikoff found that (1) deterioration of the body structure and (2) old age are (3) due to minute quantities of poisonous substances in the blood.

His book, "Prolongation of Life," furnished the first logical theory in modern times of the degeneration changes occurring in the body, and why. His findings have since been confined by leading researchers, including such prominent doctors as Carrel, Crile and Empringham.

1. Crile said, "There is no actual death. All deaths from so-called natural causes are merely the end-points of a progressive acid saturation."
2. Empringham said, "All creatures automatically poison themselves. Not time but these toxic products (in the blood) produce the senile changes that we call old age."
3. Carrell asserted, "The cell is immortal. It is merely the fluid in which it floats that degenerates. Renew this fluid at proper intervals, and give the cell proper nourishment upon which to feed, and, so far as we know, the pulsation of life (in the body) may go on forever.... Quickly, involuntarily the thought comes: Why not with man? Why not purge the body of the worn-out fluids, develop a similar technique for renewing them – and so win immortality" (in the flesh)? – Man the Unknown.

Carrel was great, but he missed some vital points. He could not shake off the medical myth of cell nutrition. We show in our work, "Facts of Nutrition," that the body cells are composed of molecules, which are composed of atoms, which are composed of electrons, which are whirling centers of electricity, and that in order to nourish the cell, we would have to nourish the component parts of the cell.

Nothing but Astral Force can nourish the cell because the cell is constituted of Astral Force.

Then why must man eat gross physical food? That question we have answered in "Facts of Nutrition."

Right in the attempt to nourish the body lies the error that hurries man to the grave. Feeding hastens the degenerative process, whereas fasting quickens the process of rejuvenation.

Carrel's experiments confirmed Metchnikoff's findings: That decrepitude and early death are due to poisons in the blood. Purge the blood of its poisons, said Carrel, and the blood becomes the flowing Fountain of Youth.

PHYSICAL LIFE

"The human frame as a machine is perfect. It contains within itself no marks by which we can possibly predict its decay. It is apparently intended to go on forever" (Professor William Monroe).

Was man made to suffer somatic death? Why do some persons die at the age of 10 and 20 and sooner, while others live 100 and 150 years?

In 1904 Harry Gaze wrote a book entitled "How to Live Forever." He held that the living organism is potentially immortal and no physiological law necessitates somatic death. He said: "The cause of somatic death, or death of the body as a whole, is simple and may be completely avoided. Old age, which is somatic death partially consummated, can also be prevented. It is possible for every person so to control the vital energies that perpetual youth, accompanied by perfect health, may be realized."

Gaze seemed to think the entire problem was solved by controlling "The vital energies." He could not see that a hostile climate and a discordant environment are factors which weaken and destroy the body regardless of all control of "the vital energies."

His limited views of the subject give little practical information to him who is searching for ways and means to avoid somatic death or to lengthen the physical life span.

The world may be impressed by the doctrine itself, but in the absence of definite instructions for putting it into effect, the doctrine has no practical value.

WHY DO WE AGE

Locating and removing the basic cause of somatic death is the only solution, but Gaze said little relative to the factors that combine and produce the cause of somatic death.

The world has come to believe by experience that man does well to live 80 or 90 years. But experience is only that which has been, not necessarily that which should be.

The purpose of Life is to produce, not to destroy. The power to produce includes the power to sustain. As Life is immortal, that which it produces and sustains should be immortal, and would be were there no damaging factors beyond its control.

Cosmic Life produces man and brings him to maturity. No matter how long he may then live, his body should not, under the law, show any change to a declining trend. As the body is constantly being rebuilt, and renewed, and is never more than seven years old, biologists declare man should live 300 years and more.

As time is an error of the senses, so Old Age is an error of the understanding.

A living body cannot grow old in years, as it is being constantly repaired and renewed. But it can grow decrepit. What we mean by Old Age is decrepitude.

In discussing Time in relation to man, biologists consider four kinds of ages, to-wit:

1. Chronological (solar) age;
2. Psychological age;
3. Physiological age;
4. Pathological age.

The first is the number of years man lives as calculated by the revolution of the earth on its axis. The second represents his brain development as disclosed by his mental processes. The third refers to his physical development, and fourth deals with his deterioration.

There is actually no age. Time is only a conception of the mind. Eternity is now, the Eternal Now is the state in which we are. It is infinite duration. In Eternity we always are.
Man's duration (chronological age) is expressed in units of Solar time, measured by the motion of the hands of a clock that registers the speed of the earth's revolution on its axis and around the sun.

Physiological and Solar Time begin for the living body when it is born, and end in the somatic death of that particular body.

Birth into the present is death as we leave the previous life; and death in the present is birth as we enter the Future Life (John 3:3).

Man's internal time is divided into three phases; psychological, physiological and pathological.

WHY DO WE AGE

Certain of man's mental activities are not modified by duration or Solar Time. They depend on the condition of the brain, and deterioration as the brain decays.

Man's internal time is as distinct from, and independent of, extrinsic (solar) time, as his body is, in space, distinct from and independent of the earth and the moon.

Man's physiological activities are not modified by duration or solar time. His state of deterioration is not the work of solar time. Internal time cannot properly be measured in units of solar time.

Chronological age in man does not correspond to physiological age. Some men remain active for years, while others grow decrepit in early life.

Pathological age in man does not correspond to chronological age. Some men are vigorous at an advanced age, while others are physical and mental wrecks while young in years or units of solar time.

Man is swept onward by the stream of physical time, not solar time. Physiological time is usually referred to as physical time, inasmuch as man's body is part of the physical world. But physical time is foreign to him, whereas internal time is his physical self.

Solar time is a uniform and constant rate. Its pace never changes. Not so with internal time. At some periods, the progress of age seems to cease, while at others it accelerates. As a rule, there is little change in the body from its 20th to its 40th year, while marked changes usually occur from its 50th to its 70th year. Most men seem to sink fast after their 70th year.

Internal time is partly suspended in hibernating animals. A similar state occurs in man during periods of fasting. This constrains biologists to believe that if man could be made to hibernate, or fast, from time to time, it would preserve health and promote longevity.

This phase of the question was tested on living cells removed from a chicken's heart. When their volume was prevented from increasing by controlled feeding, they did not show signs of age, and appeared to be immortal. It was otherwise with cells well-fed.

This demonstrable fact destroys another pet medical theory, that man should be "well nourished". Frugal feeding and fasting promote health and prolong life.

Man becomes decrepit and appears to age because in the course of years his body suffers degenerative changes due to hostile climate, unsuitable environment, and bad habits. His tissues and organs lose fluid. They become encumbered with foreign matter and connective fibers, producing hardening of tissues, organs and blood vessels.

Circulation of body fluids and nerve force is then retarded. Degeneration modifications occur in the glands. Epithelial cells lose their normal qualities by degrees.

These are some of the symptoms that constitute Old Age. They are not the work of Time.

Man's duration and decay are not ruled by Solar Time. They depend on physical, chemical, physiological and pathological factors. His body is constantly being deteriorated by his habits and environment.

As man fails to improve his habits and continues to live in an evil environment, he steadily sinks toward the grave.

FOUNTAIN OF YOUTH

"A continuous change goes on in the substance of the body and its organs, by which their materials are constantly decomposed and constantly renewed. Throughout the whole frame, vital force is incessantly engaged in taking apart the tissues of the body composition, and in building them over again of new, fresh materials, so that the tissues of the body are accordingly always renewed and always ready to perform their allotted work." – J. C. Dalton, M.D.

One of the achievements of science is the discovery within the Living Organism of the Fountain of Youth. Where else should we look for it when we are definitely told that the "Kingdom of God is within you" (Luke 17:21).

The recently discovered law of physiology, well-known to the Ancient Masters, has supplied us with a working knowledge of the secret of Perpetual Youth.

Being endowed with the Fountain of Youth, the Living Organism cannot voluntarily depart from the state of Perpetual Youth. But just as a child can sicken and die the same as an aged adult, so the organism can sink into decrepitude despite the fact that its cells and organs are always renewed and always in a state of Perpetual Youth.

The new knowledge shows that a condition of Old Age does not exist. Nor do the organs and parts of the body wear out as science claims.

Thomas Parr died in 635 at the age of 152. His body was carefully dissected by Harvey, physician to the King of England, who found no signs of decay in any organ.

Life and Matter are eternal. They are not born, nor do they die. Birth and Death are terms that express changes, not beginnings and endings. They are terms not properly applicable to the body, but to its processes.

Professor Weismann declared that Death is an acquired state that arises from conditions over which the Living Organism has no control. Such as smoking, drinking, gluttony, sexual excess, etc.

WHY DO WE AGE

Newton wrote: "Man, at his creation, was endowed with the power of perceptual youth; that is, he was formed to enjoy health, not to be a sickly, suffering creature as we now see him."

Professor Crew, Edinburgh University, said: "Science and religion affirm that in the future mankind may not only remain permanently youthful, but also may live forever" in the flesh.

Professor Monit, of Harvard, in his book, Age, Growth and Decay, says, "Death is not a universal accompaniment of Life. In many of the lower organisms death does not occur so far as we know at the present, as a natural necessary result of life. Death with them is purely the result of accident, some external cause. Our existing science leads us to the conclusion, therefore, that death has been acquired during the progress of evolution of living organisms."

In "The Science of Life" Wells and Huxley wrote: "living matter is potentially immortal. If one keeps a culture from the tissues of a young animal and takes sub-cultures regularly, the race of cells can apparently go on growing and dividing indefinitely/"

Professor J. B. Haldane, noted English Astronomer, said: "Living is actually a struggle for pure air. Keep the vast lung surface of the body supplied with fresh, unpolluted air, and also observe all other health rules, and there is scientifically speaking, no known reason why you should ever die."

In his "Believe it or Not," Ripley stated: "Numas De Cugna of Bengal, India, lived to be 370 years old. He grew four new sets of teeth, and his hair turned from grey to black four times. He died in 1566."

Arphazed, grandson of Noah, lived only 68 years longer than Cugna, dying at the age of 438 (Gen. 11:13).

In spite of the fact that the living organism cannot depart from the state of Perpetual Youth, it can suffer a condition of deterioration, and that is the condition called Old Age.

The chief object is to prevent degeneration. There is the point where medical art dismally fails. Carrel wrote: "How can we prevent the degeneracy of man?" – Man, The Unknown, P. S. It can never be done with vaccines, serums, drugs, etc.

Man is not made to degenerate. To prevent degeneration is possible and everything is certainly within the limits of that possibility. When that is accomplished, Eternal Somatic Existence and Eternal Knowledge becomes a reality instead of a dream.

The symptoms of degeneration are not "diseases." The condition called Old Age is a symbol of degeneration. The condition called somatic death is the sequel of degeneration.

WHY DO WE AGE

Man never died of disease. There is no disease per se. If man live 500 years and die of what is called Old Age, death is the result of degeneration. Old Age is a condition, not an entity.

The Living Organism contains the Fountain of Youth because it is perfectly equipped with practically unlimited powers of adaptation, self-renewal, self-repair, and self-rejuvenation. Regardless of the period of time man lives, his organism, cannot grow old. But it can degenerate.

We gain longevity when we locate the cause of degeneration and remove it. That cannot be done by studying the symptoms of degeneration and treating them as destructive entities.

Degeneration must be controlled through the Living Stream that turns the Wheels of Life. For the condition of the flesh depends upon the condition of the blood.

Pollute the blood and we plunge the body into degeneration. Pollute it more, and the body's function becomes an appalling convulsion, which in time ends in somatic death.

You may be pale, weak, anemic; you may be suffering from cancer, consumption, ulcer, tumor, or other terrible ailment; but when normal blood begins to flow through the body, all parts begin to show improvement.

PHYSIOLOGICAL TIME

Solar Time per se is foreign to the Living Organism and has no effect on it. Physiological (Internal) Time is man's own physical self. It relates to his organic development. It is measured not by Solar Time (years) but by the state of man's physical condition.

Internal Time is the expression of the changes in the body in the course of its existence. It is a fixed dimension, consisting of the series of all the organic changes that take place in man's organism from the beginning of his embryonic development to his physical demise.

These changes occur in the cells, of which the body and all its organs and glands are composed. Consequently, these changes affect the entire body.

The organism is developed from the Parent Cell by the multiplication and differentiation of billions of cells. They increase in number by the division of the pre-existing cells into two equal parts, and each part possesses similar properties.

Each new cell has a definite life-history. It grows, performs its function, and ceases to exist by dividing to form two new cells, or by disintegrating and passing from the body as waste. This waste does not pass off thru the bowels as feces, but is eliminated as gases and fluids.

44

WHY DO WE AGE

1. In growing children, the multiplication-rate of the cells exceeds the disintegration-rate, and the organism increases in size.
2. In maturity, growth ceases because these two rates become equal in all parts and structures of the body.
3. Then there comes a time when the rate of disintegration exceeds that of multiplication, and a condition of decrepitude appears.

The symptoms of the decrepit condition are termed Old Age. The body slowly sinks down in a degenerative process. Its vitality lessens and its functions decline.

The reason why degeneration begins does not appear in the organism. It is much easier to describe the symptoms termed Old Age than to discover the cause that produces the symptoms.

The symptoms come not of their own accord. They appear as the effect of a definite cause. If that cause could be discovered and removed, physiological time should be suspended. During such suspension, the organism would remain in a state of equilibrium. It would retain its normal state and function, and that would be Perpetual Youth and Eternal Physical Existence.

A definite conclusion so easily reached, so logically analyzed, and so consistently explained, should reveal that course necessary for man to attain the desired goal.

The striking differences between the living organism and a man-made machine which science ignores, lies in the fact that the organism is constantly being taken apart and rebuilt and renewed. No machine could wear out when so treated.

In every part, organ and gland of the body a continuous change is constantly occurring, by which the tissues are incessantly disintegrated, dissolved, and eliminated as waste unfit for further use. At the same time the tissues are just as constantly rebuilt and renewed. Science knows this, and yet science is so inconsistent that it says the body and its organs wear out.

The history of physiology is that of incessant change, by which the various parts and organs of the body are continuously dissolved and renewed, while the body itself should remain in a state of equilibrium, always vigorous and unaltered.

That easy it is to explain, scientifically the perfect physiological state of the organism which appears possible of attainment. Yet science seems unable to visualize and explain the means and methods by which that condition may be achieved.

The physiological processes of the body are so simple and perfect, that it is not difficult for man to keep his body always vigorous and unaltered.

WHY DO WE AGE

Science admits that the body contains no marks nor evidence by which it can predict its decay. The body is apparently intended to go on forever. The reason why it fails to do so must be found outside the body: for it is not within the body.

Various tests have shown that body cells are immortal. Man's body is a mass of cells. According to law, man should progress to Perpetual Youth by virtues of the power and quality inherent in his cells. Regardless of the fact that man may be 80 or 90 when he dies, the tissues and bones of the body are never more than one to seven years old.

The cells of an adult begin to record solar time as soon as the waste products of internal disintegration begin to accumulate and stagnate. This alters the internal state of the body. Excessive eating is one of the basic causes.

The rhythm of physiological time depends on the relation between the cells and their medium, which medium varies according to the volume, the chemical composition of the fluid and the gaseous media. When these become abnormal, they adversely affect the cells. Then in due process appear senescence and somatic death.

It seems to be the rate of accumulation of the waste products and their character, which determine the nature of the duration of the tissues.

Fasting and frugal eating reduce and remove the accumulation of waste materials. But these measures cannot offset the damage the body may suffer from a hostile environment.

The average man knows not what a hostile environment is. It is one that makes it necessary for man to build artificial shelter and depend on artificial heat to protect his body from the destructive elements.

A naked animal with tender skin is not made to live in a region where artificial covering for the body, artificial shelter and artificial heat are imperative to keep that animal from freezing to death.

A deep secret of Nature is concealed in the fact that no part of the Adamite period is so strongly painted as the Warm Climate. Man's dwelling naked in his Edenic Garden proves there was no alternative of Summer and Winter, but one war season of perpetual growth (Gen. 2:25).

If man lived as he should, under ideal conditions that met all the requirements of his body, his body should maintain its equilibrium, and at the age of 100 he should feel and be the same as he was at 30.

THE PERFECT MACHINE

"The human frame, as a machine, is perfect. It contains within itself no marks by which we can possibly predict its decay. It is apparently intended going on forever." – Monroe.

Harry Gaze in his book, "How to Live Forever," said:
"The body literally and completely returns to dust in less than one year; and during that period a new body is constructed, molecule by molecule. The question may be asked, 'Why does the body ever manifest age if it is thus renewed?' With the advance of years, there is a gradual but positive cessation of the vitality expressed, resulting, not from the years, but from the failure of the individual to co-operate with the process of renewal."

We need definite details instead of vague generalizations in order to know exactly what to do to accomplish the results desired.

It is not the effect of the earth's turning on its axis that changes the body. Nor is it the body itself where we should search for that cause which sends man to the grave regardless of whether he has lived few or many years.

Herbert Spencer thought he was on the right road when he wrote, "perfect correspondence would be perfect life. Were there no changes in the environment but such as the organism had adapted changes to meet, and were it never to fail in the efficiency with which it met them, that would be Eternal Existence and Eternal Knowledge."

We now have something definite to consider. Spencer was not wrong when he believed that Environment is the governing factor; but he was decidedly wrong in assuming that the Living Organism could come into physical being in an environment so hostile to its constitution, that such environment contained adverse conditions which the organism had not adapted changes to meet. That theory may satisfy the Evolutionist but not the Naturist.

The Naturist knows that it was a condition of perfect correspondence as between the organism and its environment which made possible the physical actuality of the organism.

A fertile egg contains a potential chick; but that potentially never can become a reality until transformed into such by the power inherent in a perfect environment.

There is nothing new under the sun. That which hath been is that which shall be (Eccl. 1:9). The germ of man always existed potentially or he could never exist actually. That potential man never become an actual man until transformed into actuality by the power inherent in a perfect environment.

It is an exhibition of ignorance of basic biological facts for one to assert that the Living Organism could come into actual existence in an environment beset with conditions with which the organism was not in perfect harmony. For such harmony was a condition precedent to man's physical appearance.

Man will advance any excuse to hide his errors before he will admit that no sooner had he appeared as an actual physical entity, than his evil work began to change his perfect environment, producing adverse conditions which his body had not adapted changes to meet.

That great scientist Carrel recognized this fact. He wrote: "The environment that molded the body and the soul of our ancestors during many milleniums has now been replaced by another. This silent revolution has occurred almost without our noticing it. We have not realized its importance. But it is one of the most dramatic events in human history. For any modification in their surroundings inevitably and profoundly disturbs all living beings.

"The modern city consists of monstrous edifices and of dark, narrow streets full of gasoline fumes, coal dust, and toxic gases, torn by the noise of taxicabs, trucks, and trollys, and thronged ceaselessly by great crowds. Obviously, it has not been planned for the good of its inhabitants.

"The natural conditions of existence have been destroyed by modern civilization" (Man, The Unknown. Pp. 10, 25, 29).

There is the story in a few words. Man destroys himself by his own work... As soon as he came into physical being he began building centers of destruction. Cain is mentioned in the Bible as the first to build a city (Gen. 4:17).

Passing from its environment to the organism itself, it must be considered that physical maturity is not the finality of the organism. It is only a limitation on individual size and strength. It is that point where equilibrium appears in the multiplication-rate and disintegration-rate of the cells.

As long as equilibrium prevails, there is a balance, under the law of change, between cell disintegration and reintegration, making possible the conditions of degeneration, decrepitude, old age. If that state of equilibrium remained constant and changed not, Eternal Existence and Eternal Knowledge would be the result.

Within the body itself is the power that establishes and maintains perfect and permanent equilibrium between the processes of anabolism and catabolism-- destruction and construction. That is the Fountain of Youth. But that power of the body is disrupted by the evil effect of an adverse environment and bad habits.

A body that is constantly being rebuilt and renewed, cannot grow old and wear out. If a machine were incapable of wearing out, it would be incapable of coming to an end, without an accident. So the body is incapable of wearing out, and with proper environment and proper care, it should never come to an end, barring accidents.

In certain respects, the living organism may be compared to a steam engine, carefully constructed of the best steel, mechanically perfect operating smoothly, all parts working in harmony with one another.

We shall raise that engine up to the high plane of the living organism by giving it the same inherent, automatic, and practically unlimited powers of self-starting, self-building, self-operating, self-adjusting, self-repairing, self-renovating, self-renewing, and self-governing.

Under no circumstances could man do aught for that engine but supply it with the material it needed of the kind needed, at the time needed, and in the quantity needed, for its use, repair, renewal, etc., and that engine, at the end of a thousand years, would be the same, operating and performing the same, and be the same in every detail as in the first year of its existence. It would be as impossible for that machine to grow old, wear out, decay and fall to ruin as for the sun to rise in the west and set in the east.

The engine, no less than the human body, is governed by law, the life of the engine would soon come to an end if that law were not known and observed.

For instance, if we exposed the engine to the weather (adverse environment), fed it soft lead instead of fine steel for use in repairing its wear and tear; and in place of good oil, used water containing Sand to lubricate its bearings and joints, we know without experience that such maltreatment would soon derange its smooth operation, weaken its structure, grind out its parts, and start it rapidly on the road to ruin.

The living organism is perfectly equipped with all the powers we have given the engine. No man can do more for his body than to keep it in the proper environment, supply it with the material it needs, of the quantity and quality needed, at the time needed, and treat the body as it was intended by God to be treated.

More than this the body does not require, and more than this the body cannot receive without suffering some injury. Under these ideal conditions, there is no more reason for the body's wearing out, decaying and falling to ruin than for the engine to do so.

The human body, in the beginning if not now, was perfect; and it was then, if not now, placed in that Environment the changes of which the body was perfectly equipped with adapted changes to meet. And it would never have failed in the efficiency with which it met them, but for the interference and evil work of man, and his maltreatment of his body.

WHY DO WE AGE

PATHOLOGICAL AGE

Pathological Age, like Physiological Age, is not measured by chronological (solar) age, but by the state of man's physical condition.

Pathological age is the degenerative expression of the adverse changes in the body and its functions in the course of its existence. It is representing the degree of deterioration the body has suffered. It is a process of organic degeneration, and its symptoms are what doctors are taught to study, name and term diseases.

There is no disease per se. There is good health and bad health only.
The condition called Old Age is pathological age. It represents the state of the body, not the period of its existence.

The adverse changes in the body, its organs and glands, termed the "Work of Old Age" by the doctors, is a gradual process of deterioration. It is that state of physical decline man suffers, not because of the earth's turning on its axis, but because of –
1.   Bad Climate,
2.   Bad Environment, and
3.   Bad Habits.

The living organism cannot grow old, as so called old age is a state of degeneration that is not yet sufficiently advanced to prevent the organs from performing their function, but their function is faulty and below par.

People never die of so-called old age. Dr. Krasner searched through the records of the Institute of Pathology, Western Research University, Cleveland, Ohio, in the case of 20,000 persons whose bodies were examined after death, and not in one case had any of the doctors noted "Old Age" as the cause of death. Every victim had died of some ailment that had no relation to age.

When man's vitality begins to fade and his step to falter, he thinks he is growing old, and regards his 60 or 70 years of Solar Time as the cause of his declining. The Solar Time that has passed since his birth, and not his environment nor mode of living, he blames for his condition.

The turning of the earth on its axis sends no man to the grave. His somatic demise results from the collapse of his organs that are no longer able to perform their function. This collapse is not the work of Solar Time, but this is the effect of acute and chronic poisoning, plus the strain man constantly puts on his body by his lawless mode of living.

Vital organs are not constructed to wear out and collapse at certain times, as taught by medical art. The time when they succumb depends on the amount of strain and abuse they have suffered by reason of man's unlawful course of living.

WHY DO WE AGE

Solar Time has no place in biology and physiology, and is not an etiological factor in pathological age. Nor is it a cause of degeneration and decline.

So-called aging does take place in Time; but it is not the work of Time. It is the cumulative effect of many impairing influences that operate in and thru a period of time.

Man's health is permanently damaged and his body degenerated by the inimical influence of a hostile environment and bad habits; and he can never return to his former state of vigor and vitality.

Complete recovery from any illness, no matter how slight, is impossible. Each illness leaves its degenerative mark in the body, there to remain forever, similar to a scar on one's hand from a bad injury.

"We may recover from disease" writes the great Carrel, "but we bear forever the scar." -- Man, The Unknown. P. 170.

If man fully recovered from every ailment, there would be no physical degeneration, no decline, no decrepitude, and the body would go on forever. It is the cumulative effects of each ailment that finally sends the body to the grave.

From the day of our first cold down to the last day of life, a process of deterioration continues through the years and ends only at the grave.

Krasner found in examining a so-called worn-out heart, that a previous illness left inflamed areas and other permanent marks of damage to the internal organs. His investigation showed that each illness leaves marks of permanent damage.

The scars that each illness leaves are cumulative. They sink deeper and deeper into the tissues. Their onward march, not Solar Time, at least gives their victim a startling shock. The day comes when he realizes that he is slipping and slowing up.

Man imagines this to be the work of Solar time because the doctors so teach. But the earth's turning on its axis has no power to build degenerative changes in the body, or sap its vitality.

It is the constantly dropping water, not time, that wears away the stone. Stop the destructive action of that dropping water, and eons of Time may pass, but the stone will remain unaffected.

In the "Precepts of Ptah-hotep," contained in the Papyrus Prisse, said to be the oldest book on earth, there is forbidding picture of the miseries of "Old age" from the mouth of Ptah-hotep himself, who was then 110. He said:

"The process of decay changes into senility. Decay falls upon man and decline takes the place of youth. A vexation weighs upon him every day. Sight fails; the ear becomes deaf; the strength dissolves; the speech fails; the mind weakens; remembering not the day before. The whole body suffers. Taste disappears. The nose is stopped, breathing no more from exhaustion."

This man did not say that Solar Time is the cause of decline. He did not say it was the work of sickness or disease. He termed it "process of decay." He was right, whereas modern doctors are wrong. They term it "old age". But Ptah-hotep appeared not to know the basic cause of that decay which changes into senility.

The "process of decay" is the work of definite causes. These causes are not (1) within the organism, are not (2) due to defective construction of the organism, and are not (3) the work of Solar Time.

The definite reference to Speech fails, nose being stopped, an breathing no more from exhaustion tell a clear story to him who knows that breathing is the primal function of living, and that when man stops breathing he stops living.

As far back as we can go in human history, we find evidence that the leading cause of degeneration and decrepitude is polluted air. Yet down to this day medical text-books contain almost nothing in reference to the condition or kind of air one breathes.

Speech fails, nose fails, breathing fails when the Organs of Life have deteriorated so extensively from the effects of polluted air that they can no longer inhale enough of the Breath of Life to supply the body's needs.

Now we shall notice some of the degenerative changes in the body of a man who always appeared to have good health. Of course he suffered from that slight ailment termed the common cold, just as the doctors and all other people do, but just like the doctors, he did not consider that anything serious.

This man was struck by a motor car and rushed to a hospital, where he died within an hour. In view of the statement of the man's wife that he was always in good health, the doctors decided to make an autopsy of the body. This is what they found:

1. Scar tissues in both lungs (work of polluted air);
2. Hardening of liver and arteries;
3. Heart enlargement;
4. Chronic kidney trouble (principally from salt eating) but enough kidney tissue left to perform the necessary function despite destruction of portions of both kidneys.
5. Based on the condition of his organs, the doctors assumed the man, also had high blood pressure.

This was the condition of the body of a man who had never been sick. With all this degeneration of his organs, the common condition of man in civilization, the victim was active and vigorous, and believed himself in good health. He may have gone farther, as many ignorant people do, and declared that he was in "perfect health." The average adult in civilization knows nothing about good health. He knows nothing about a thing he never saw, or a condition he never had.

DECREPITUDE

The doctors like to tell us that the body wears out like a man-made machine. Again, the doctors are wrong.

The condition the doctors term Old Age is Pathological Age – a state of Decrepitude. Man comes into being and passes thru the several stages of infancy, childhood, youth, adulthood, and then sinks into decrepitude – provided the doctors do not send him to the grave before that condition has time to develop.

Decrepitude results from a gradual increase in density and firmness of the bones, cartilages, tendons, ligaments, membranes, tissues and all the organs and glands.

The joints become stiff and ache. They grate when moved. The synovial fluid that lubricates and keeps them flexible when we are young, is diminished in quantity and rendered too thick and glutinous to serve its purpose.

All parts, organs and glands partake of the same hardening process. There is no hardening of the arteries, as the doctors claim, while the rest of the body remains soft and flexible.

Millions of minute capillary vessels, which ramify the spread thru the entire body like the branches of a tree, gradually clog up and change into solid fiber, no longer pervious to the blood. The tiny cells of the lungs suffer the same fate, the air can no longer enter them, and symptoms of this condition are shortness of breath and difficulty in breathing.

The body, once elastic, healthy, alert, pliable, active and sensitive, becomes stiff, slow, insensible. Finally, the body dies of some ailment which it was able to throw off when it was more vital. The many cases of influenza thru the years left the body weaker and weaker, and finally the body succumbed.

The chief difference between the body of old age and childhood is the greater density and rigidity caused by greater proportions of calcerous, earthy substance entering into the body's composition.

The bones of a child are composed of three parts of gelatine to one of mineral matter. In old age this proportion is reversed. That makes it important to discover the source of this destructive accumulation of hardening matter.

Analysis shows that the blood carries earthy substances of the same kind as the solidifying agents; but the arterial blood flowing out over the body from the heart, contains more earthy matter than the venous blood flowing back to the heart.

This shows that, in every cycle the blood leaves some earthy substance, and this earthy substance is what clogs and hardens the system.

That knowledge makes the solution simple. Man should partake of such air, liquid and food as will deposit the least amount of hardening matter in the tissues, and also keep the eliminative organs active.

Air comes first because it is entering the body constantly from birth to death. In life magazine of February 12th, 1951, appeared an article headed "SMOG", and the author said: "Every time a New Yorker takes a breath, he inhales 69,000 particles of grit and dust. His lungs are black."

Almost everywhere in the United States and city dweller lives in a sea of coal-grime, sulphuric acid, ammonia, carbon and other aerial garbage that is generally called "smog".

"Smog irritates the mucous membrane lining the respiratory tract, causing people to choke up and cough violently. The result of this is a partial 'drowning' in the body's own excessive excretions of fluids." When people die of influenza, pneumonia, or any lung ailment, their lungs have become a solid mass that prevents the entrance of air. That solid mass results from excessive excretions of fluids in the lungs to wash away the irritants and poisons that enter the lungs at each inhalation. The result is the same as filling the lungs with water, as when one drowns. Air cannot enter the lungs, breathing stops, and that is the end.

Water from the ground should never enter the body. For it contains minerals in solution that settle in the tissues and cause them to harden.

The lungs, skin and urinary systems are the saviors of man from an early grave. But for their eliminative work, no one could live longer than ten years under the health-destroying conditions of civilization.

It is estimated that common, undistilled water from the ground contains carbonate and other compounds of lime to such extent, that the average quantity of water used each day by one person in the form of tea, coffee, soup and drink, would be sufficient to form a block of solid stones the size of a large man in thirty years.

Phosphate of lime is always found in the urine of adults, but not in that of children, as the rapid formation of bone in children requires that this mineral be retained. And it is largely an excess of this mineral entering the body that hastens growth, maturity, and decrepitude.

In ordinary cases, earthy matter is much in evidence in the urine of adults, and due to this fact is one reason why physical life reaches even its present short length. If the earthy matter were not eliminated by the kidneys, decrepitude and somatic death had come much sooner.

Undistilled water from the ground, taken internally comes next to polluted air to being one of man's worst enemies.

WHY DO WE AGE

Rain water, caught before coming in contact with the earth, is distilled water and free of the hardening minerals that ruin the body.

The kidneys are also active in eliminating the ashes of the body. But despite the great amount of earth deposits eliminated in the urine, enough remains in many cases to form gravel and stone in bladder, kidneys and liver.

Be not deceived that water contains less hardening minerals because of being boiled. Notice how stone forms on the sides and bottom of the tea kettle, left there by the evaporated water. Boiling evaporates the water but leaves the earthy matter behind.

Hardened tissues and blood vessels are improved by drinking distilled water and juices of fruits and vegetables. But the distilled water also leaches out the minerals of the teeth, causing them to crumble and decay. This is not so in the case of rain water, snow and hail, as such water is changed with minerals from the air that the body needs and uses.

Flesh eating does the body less harm than tubers and grains, as they contain much earthy matter. Fruits, berries, melons, tomatoes, and leafy vegetables, eaten without any kind of seasoning, are the natural food of man. They contain all the mineral salts and body needs, but not the earthy matter that hardens the body.

Hilton Hotema

SCIENTIFIC LIVING

RECUPERATION

Recuperation here means recovery from illness.

All recovery from illness were impossible if the Living Organism was not so definitely constituted that it can never function otherwise except in the one direction of normal healthy. It cannot reverse its process and function in the opposite direction, despite the absured claims of medical art to the contrary.

But it is possible for the organism to destroy itself in its struggle to overcome the obstacles in its path-- as filling the lungs so full of blood and mucus that breathing becomes exceedingly difficult or entirely impossible.

This process is a protective measure. The mucus is poured out in the lungs to protect the lung-cells from and to wash away the deadly irritants that enter the lungs with the air one breathes.

The struggle can well be termed a battle to the death. For that is exactly what it is. It occurs in the case of influenza or pneumonia, when the lungs become congested with blood, rushed there by the body's governing forces to furnish a flood of mucus for the purpose stated.

In this death struggle, as the body strives to protect itself from the poisonous irritants in the air, the lungs become so full of blood and mucus that breathing is impossible and death ensues, just as when the lungs are filled with water when one drowns.

There is one safe and effective remedy to relieve the congested condition and it must be applied quickly.

The vast blood vascular system of the skin must be expanded by a hot bath, to create a vacuum that draws the excess blood from the lungs and decreases there the excessive excretion of mucus.

The Recuperative Powers of the Organism do their work efficiently and affectively when properly aided by strictly natural measures, as fasting and heating, thus giving these powers unobstructed opportunity to perform their function properly.

While a big book could not adequately cover this phase of physiology, and as one case is sufficient to show what is possible in millions of other cases, we shall cite some instances to show what a dangerous nuisance and hindrance the orthodox doctors are to their patients' recovery, and how effectively the body takes care of itself when given a chance.

1. The press of March 13th, 1948, stated that William A. Rutledge of St. Louis, Missouri, "consulted a physician 65 years ago about a lung ailment. After calling in four other doctors, the physician told Rutledge they all agreed that he had only about a year to live." The

frightened Rutledge turned from the physicians to Mother Nature, and what happened? What the doctors did not want to happen, but what a naturist would expect to happen. The account continues:

"Rutledge celebrated his 93rd birthday today with a brisk workout at the downtown Y.M.C.A. The spry old gent, a retired real estate dealer, did some calisthenics, tossed a medicine ball around, and said it was good to have the first 93 years behind him".

What about those five physicians who gave Rutledge one year to live? The account said "All of the five doctors are dead."

"Physician, heal thyself" (Luke 4:23)

2. John Bailes, of England, in middle life suffered from a severe illness of a chronic nature. The physicians were unable to help him. They told him that he could not get well and had only a short time to live. Bailes then turned to Mother Nature, adopted a healthful mode of living, and many years after all those physicians were dead, he died at the age of 128.

    "Physician, heal thyself".

3. The recuperative powers of the body are strikingly illustrated in the case of Ludovico Carnaro, a Venetian nobleman, born in 1467.

WHY DO WE AGE

According to the history of his case, at the age of 25 Cornaro became a chronic drunkard. At the age of 40 he was a physical and mental wreck. The physicians told him repeatedly that he could not live. He then quit drinking, turned to mother Nature, and regained health to such extent that he lived to be 103.

Cornaro became the greatest of modern food experts. He found that a simple diet of 12 ounces of solid food and 16 ounces of unfermented wine daily was best for him. With the exception of twelve years, he lived on this ration for over 63 years. Within one year he had recovered health. His wife adopted the same course, and bore children very late in life. She also lived beyond the century mark. (See, HOW TO LIVE 100 YEARS By Cornaro.)

On his 78th birthday, Cornaro's friends urged him to increase his ration. Reluctantly he agreed to a 14-ounce allowance. In twelve days he was stricken with fever, with pain in his right side. At once he returned to the 12-ounce ration, but suffered for 35 days.

That was his only illness in 63 years. He wrote several books, the last after the age of 95. In his book entitled "Birth and Death of Man," he said of himself: "I am now as healthy as a person of 25. I write daily six or seven hours, and the rest of the time I occupy in walking, conversing, and occasionally attending concerts. I am happy. My imagination is lively, my memory tenacious, my judgment good, and what is most remarkable in a person of my advanced age, my voice is strong and harmonious."

(Note: Hotema is 81 and has not been ill for 70 years; and you who read his writings may judge for yourself whether his Mind and Memory are in good condition. He is up before daylight, walking and running in the fresh morning air, doing these things while it is still dark, for if people saw him doing such "silly stunts," they would think he was nuts.)

The secret of Cornaro's strong voice to the last lies in the fact that he did not live in and breathe the polluted air of our civilization.

4. We now come to the exceptional case of Goddard E. Diamond, born in Plymouth, Mass., May 11, 1796. He moved to San Francisco, Calif., in 1877 and died there of pneumonia in 1916 at the age of 120. Polluted air finally killed him.

In 1915 Dr. M. Thrasher published a book titled "Long Life in California," in which he said: "Captain Diamond lives at Crocker Old Peoples' Home in San Francisco. I have personally known him for 23 years, since he was 96; and today he seems no older."

WHY DO WE AGE

When he was 79 Diamond suffered from a serious case of hardened tissues and blood vessels, with stiffness of the joints. Yet for years he had been a strict vegetarian. Some authorities told that grains and tubers do the body more damage than flesh.

The muscles of Diamond's legs and back were so stiff, he could not rise from a chair nor sit down without great discomfort, and he often required the aid of an assistant. The tissues of his arms and hands were so stiff, that it was hard for him to hold knife and fork to feed himself.

Orthodox physicians were unable to help him, and pronounced his case incurable. They told him he could not get well and had but a short time to live.

That information would scare almost any one, and it scared Diamond. There was nothing now for him to do but turn to Nature, as he should have done in the first place. He adopted a healthful mode of living, and many years after all those doctors were dead and buried, Diamond died at the age of 120.

When Diamond was past the age of 100, he was doing gymnastic work with an athletic club that few young men could equal. At the age of 108 he was riding a bicycle and walking 20 miles a day. He attended social events, and when he was 110 he danced most of the evening on the occasion with an athletic girl of 16.

As history is replete with accounts of such cases, none of which are of any interest to medical art, it constrains one to ask, "How long could man live if he began before he was a physical wreck to live right, and so continued to the end?"

While damaged heart, liver, kidneys, stomach, may be regenerated to the extent that they fail to trouble the owner, and may give fair service for years, the damaged organs can never again become normal. A wound or any part of the body will be repaired, but it leaves a scar composed of low grade tissue that can never function normally.

A fatty heart, a fibrous liver, a deranged stomach – these damaged organs cannot return to their normal state. But as the original size of an external scar diminishes with the years, so the damaged organs, by more healthful living, will improve with the years.

Diamond's case supplies splendid evidence to show that vegetarianism, as practiced by most people, is not the penacea it is believed by many to be. As a vegetarian, his diet consisted of cereal products, tubers, with some fruit and green vegetables. Yet at 79 he was a chronic invalid.

Complete recovery from any ailment is a myth. If one recovered fully as the doctors believe, it is obvious to an intelligent person that physical decline would be impossible, and man would never suffer somatic death.

Each illness results from internal poisoning, and each time there is permanent, internal damage that decreases one's vitality. The decrease is so slight as not to be noticeable may be for years. But too soon comes the sad day when it is painfully apparent and the victim feels his vitality fading.

If man knew what to do and would do it, he could check the declining process to a certain extent and add years to his lifespan. But how can the common man know when even the best doctors don't know? If they did, instead of dying as they do at the ages of 50 and 60, they would do it for themselves. For they love life no less than the lawyer or the layman.

As bad climate, bad environment, and bad habits constitute the basic cause, the only remedy on earth is good climate, good environment and good habits.

If medical art knew this, it would never let such precious knowledge become general, as that would lead to a world of health, and such a world would ruin not only the doctors, but all that long list of workers and institutions that thrive on human misery.

It is the effect of internal poisoning that produces each siege of sickness, and each time there is a slight loss of vitality that is never regained as the doctors think.

A time is certain to come when the cumulative effect of that lost vitality grows great enough to be apparent, and the decrepitude that ensues shows man that he is definitely declining.

The alarm seizes the victim, and the sinking process is hastened by the destructive measures taken to halt it. The misinformed victim takes tonics and stimulants on the doctor's orders, and these poisonous products do nothing but hurry the sufferer to the grave.

FRUGAL FEEDING

All tests and experiments show that eating is harmful to a certain extent, regardless of what one eats. Two pens of rats were put on a feeding test. One pen was fed in the regular way, and the other fasted one day in three. The latter rats lived 727 days, while those fed in the regular way died in 650 days.

Another test was made. It was termed "Studies in Underfeeding." What doctor has the courage to advice "underfeeding"? If he did, he'd be considered crazy. People must be "well-nourished" or bad things can be expected. The "underfeeding" test was made on two pens of rats. One pen was fed in the regular way and the rats died in 650 days. The other pen was fed on a diet considered deficient in certain elements the doctors say one must have or suffer serious consequences.

This diet was considered deficient in calories. The rats did not grow so fast, but they lived 1105 days – or 70 percent longer than the rats fed in the regular way. The test showed that rapid growth portends rapid decay and early death. This is true in both plants and animals. Yet parents want their children to grow fast.

Overeating produces various disorders, rapid growth, and short life.

What constitutes over-eating? The amount of food eaten by those who have access to all they can eat, and made more tasty by the cook to promote gluttony. Three big meals per day is over-eating; yet that is eating according to doctors orders. Most people eat not only three big meals per day, but much between meals. At regular meal-time they may not be hungry, but eat for fear something bad may happen if they don't.

The doctors declare that it is inviting danger to miss a meal. That failing appetite shows something bad is brewing in the body, and the appetite should be whipped up with a tonic.

Doctors are not expected to give attention to health measures, for they live and thrive on human ailments. A world of health would ruin them.

This is a good time and place to mention the case of George Hasler Johnson, who hiked miles without eating to win $1,000 offered by the late Bernarr Macfadden, editor and publisher of Physical Culture Magazine. Johnson started in Chicago June 1, 1926, and ended his hike at Bald Knob, Pa., on June 20. His failure to go on to New York City, original destination, was due to the condition of his feet.

He hiked nearly 600 miles in 20 days through storm, wind and sunshine, through burning heat and under many difficulties, and not a morsal of food passed his lips.

Of the condition of his feet, he said: "Tortured nature demanded rest. The tissues were worn from my feet by the thousands of steps I had taken over burning pavements, and the delicate bones that form the arches were unprotected. This caused me excruciating pain. At last I had to stop. "Physical Culture, Aug. 1926, p. 30.

Macfadden paid him the $1,000.

Every test proves that frugal feeding promotes health and prolongs life. The tests prove that self-denial in all things is the Path to Perfection.

The less man uses and indulges, the more perfect he becomes. He gains in perfection as he gains freedom from desires and appetites.

Therefore, "If any man will come after me (Perfection), let him deny himself and follow me". (Mat. 16:24). In other words, he that overcometh all desires and appetites and masters himself, shall inherit all things good in life, and Perfection will be his State of Being, supplying him with Good Health and Long Life in his own right, as the reward he has earned.

It is the law of cause and effect: Whatsoever man soweth, that shall he also reap. (Gal. 6:7).

REJUVENATION

His flesh shall be fresh as a child's; he shall return to the days of his youth (Job. 33:25). These things worketh nature often time with man (Job. 33:29). And they youth shall be renewed like the eagle's (Psalms 103:5).

The great Dr. Carrel believed in Rejuvenation, but did not believe in the methods used by Steinach and Voronoff in their attempts to make old man young. They thought that senility resulted from deficient gonad glands. Carrel wrote:

"The loss of activity of the sexual glands is not the case of senescence but one of its consequences. It is possible that neither Steinach nor Voronoff had ever observed true rejuvenation. But their failure does not by any means signify that rejuvenation is impossible to obtain" (Man, The Unknown, P. 183).

Rejuvenation means becoming young again. That actually occurs to a certain extent when men, 28 years old as Rutledge was, 37 years old as Bailes was, 40 years old as Cornaro was, and 79 years old as Diamond was, are given up by orthodox doctors as incurable wrecks, and to a degree that they live more than a hundred years, outliving by many years the physicians who had said they would not get well and had but a short time to live.

Overwhelming evidence shows that Carrel was correct when he declared that "Our ignorance (of the body and its functions) is profound" (Man, The Unknown, P. 4).

It is far easier to hold health than to recover it when lost. But thousands of cases could be cited of those who lost their health and recovered it by leaving the physicians and turning to Mother Nature.

Since a badly deranged body is competent, under the care of Mother Nature, to regain its equilibrium and go on to the age of 128, as in the case of Bailes, then a healthy body, under the proper care of Mother Nature, should go on for several centuries, as physiologists assert it should do.

It is important to observe in the cases cited, and thousands more that could be mentioned, that the body's Recuperative

WHY DO WE AGE

Powers did their effective work only after the victims abandoned the doctors and turned to Mother Nature.

Had these men remained under the care of doctors, they would not have regained health and would have died years before they did. Daily experience proves that the destructive work of the doctors interferes with natural processes, and their "remedies" poison the blood and body more, making early death sure and certain.

Based on years of study and research, Carrel actually formulated the Law of Physical Immortality in these simple words:

> "The rhythm of Physiological Time depends on the relations between the tissues and their (fluidal) medium" (Man, The Unknown. P. 173).

Carrel listed five factors definitely involved in his formula. These are:
1. The cell is immortal;
2. The fluid in which it floats degenerates;
3. The cells show age when the fluid becomes foul;
4. Purge the body of its vitiated fluids;
5. Develop a technique for renewing the fluids, and thus win physical immortality.

Carrel's most amazing experiment was that of keeping chicken heart tissue alive in a test tube for twenty-seven years after it was removed from the foul. He showed that the living cell is immortal. Being satisfied that the cell is immortal, he then threw it away. Astounding: Physical immortality is possible.

Carrel found that the cells begin to record solar time (old age) as soon as their constantly dissolving parts begin to accumulate and stagnate, and thus alter (poison) the fluid surrounding the cells. He wrote:

"The simplest system where the phenomenon of senescence is observed, consists of a group of cells cultivated in a fluid medium. In such a system, the medium is progressively modified by the products of disintegration and, in turn, modifies the cells. Then appear senescence and death.... The rhythm of physiological time depends on the relations between the tissues and their medium. (Man, The Unknown. P. 173).

Rhythm means "measured motion", as the function of breathing, or the beating of the heart. That is the rhythm of physiological time, and has no relation to solar time.

Carrel showed that the (1) rate of accumulation of waste products in the body fluids, and (2) the nature of these products, determine (3) the characteristics of the duration of the tissues.

When the composition of the body fluids is constantly maintained in a normal state, the cells maintain their normal condition and show no signs of age. They record physiological time but no solar time. They record measured MOTION but not measured TIME.

WHY DO WE AGE

The rhythm of physiological time is not modified except by interference with certain fundamental processes and their mode of association, as by the bad habits of a man or the obstructive work of the doctor.

When the fluid surrounding the cells fails to remove promptly the dissolving parts of the cells, then the fluid changes, degenerates. This modifies the cells, and then appear senescence and death. These conditions are hastened by the poisonous remedies of the doctor.

Guided by this scientific clew, unorthodox physiologists, turning from misleading medical art and looking beyond medical text-books for the Elixir of Life, began piecing together their own findings and comparing them with the fragments of the writings of the Ancient Masters.

1. The simplicity of their initial discovery shocked them. They found that all animals, when ill, positively refuse to eat. Here is a law of Nature said they. The discovery was confusing, for medical teaching is diametrically opposed to any forms of fasting, and more especially in cases of illness. Under the theory of "medical science" that food supplies vital energy, the ill need food more than the well.

2. These unorthodox physiological men looked farther beyond the text-books of the Holy Medical Authorities, and did more thinking. They observed the high death-

rate under orthodox medical practice of feeding patients well, and they grew more skeptical.

They studied the cases of animals that invariably fast when ill, and found that the animals almost always recover health. This law of Nature works, said they.

3.   These men then studied the writings of the Ancient Masters and found frequent reference to fasting. The Masters knew the Law.

4.   Lastly, they discovered that the Masters never filled their stomach with food when preparing for unusual events. They always fasted. Not only did they know the law, but they obeyed it.

The Masters recognized Fasting as a rejuvenating Process, and resorted to it in instance of illness and on other occasions. The measure was also employed generally in ancient days to improve human health, and the rulers, by official edict, proclaimed periodic fasts throughout their realms. (2 Chron. 20:3). The Bible states:

"The word of the Lord of hosts came unto me saying: The Fast of the fourth month, and the fast of the fifth, and the fast of the sixth, and the fast of the seventh, and the fast of the tenth, shall be to the house of Judah Joy and gladness" (Zech. 8:19).

Moses fasted forty days (Ex. 24:18). Elijah fasted forty days (1 Kings 19:8). The gospel Jesus fasted forty days (Matt. 4:2). These men were natural scientists and knew how to promote health and prolong life. In their day the faith of the people had not deserted Mother Nature and centered in the doctors.

With this valuable experience as a guide, the unorthodox physiologists began experimenting on worms, with results so favorable that they turned to men. Always the same good results were obtained.

5.   By fasting their patients, recoveries of physical wrecks, of hopelessly chronic cases pronounced incurable by orthodox doctors, were so remarkable as to be astounding. The wave of enthusiasm that swept over them constrained them to term Fasting the "Wonder Cure". It was tried and tested for years by Dr. Adolph Mayer, eminent German physician, with results so startling that he wrote a book on it, in which he said:
"I positively assert that Fasting is the most efficient means known for correcting disease" (The Wonder Cure).

Then came Dr. Moeller, superintendent of the Closchwtiz Sanitarium and after much experience in fasting patients, he wrote:

"Fasting is the only natural evolutionary method whereby, through a systematic cleansing, the body can restore itself by degrees to physiological normality."

6. As so-called disease is only a condition, of degeneration, reasoned these wise unorthodox physiologists, a procedure that consistently and effectively removes the condition termed disease, and restores the body's normal physiology, must be a Process of Rejuvenation.

Overwhelming evidence proves that they were absolutely right.

That is the manner in which unorthodox physiologists discovered the Law of Rejuvenation. But medical art is not interested in improving health and saving life because it lives and thrives on human misery.

When fasting frees the internal organs of labor and strain, they at once begin to purge the body of its vitiated fluids, and this restores the rhythm of Physiological Time.

This is the recuperative process that halts the march of solar time. This is the Law of Rejuvenation.

LONGEVITY (A)

"All creatures automatically poison themselves... Not Time but these toxic products produce the senile changes that we call old age." – James Empringham, M.D.

Dr. George W. Crile, said, "There is no natural death. All deaths from so-called natural diseases are merely the end-point of a progressive acid saturation."

E. Metchnikoff, great Russian scientist, was jeered by his brethren for declaring, after years of investigation, that deterioration of the body and old age are not the work of Time. He said the conditions are due to small quantities of poisonous substances in the blood. But he could offer no reasonable solution to the problem.

His work furnished the first logical explanation in modern times of the degenerative changes that occur in the body, and why. These degenerative changes are what doctors term disease. There is a condition of bad health, of degeneration, but no disease.

There has been much speculation as to the limit set on the duration of man's life.

It is written that "his days shall be an hundred and twenty years" (Gen. 6:3); and that "the days of our years are threescore years and ten; and if by reason of strength they be four-score years" (Ps. 90:10).

According to the Bible, Abraham lived 175 years (Gen. 25:7). Isaac lived 180 years (Gen. 35:28). Jacob lived 147 years (Gen. 47:28). Joseph lived 110 years (Gen. 50:26).

In modern times men lived 160 years, 256 years, and 370 years.

The press of October 8th 1943, reported that Professor C. H. Dennesen celebrated his 110th birthday July 10th 1943. His maternal grandfather died at 112, and his paternal grandfather at 125. His sister broke the family record by dying young. She lived to be only 106.

The press of February 19th 1945, reported that "Indian Ned Rasper" was born in Siskiyou County, California, in 1826, and at the age of 119 was still active and in good health.

The press of August 19th 1943, reported that Saddi Wested, of Nagpur, India died five days before at the age of "more than 160."

The press reported the case of Li Chung-yun of China who died in 1933 at the age of 256.

According to Homer, Nestor lived 300 years, and Dando, the Illyrian, and the King of the Lacmons were said to have reached ages of five and six centuries.

WHY DO WE AGE

In view of this evidence, there is nothing extraordinary about the biblical ages of Abraham, Isaac and Jacob. The evidence also shows that the limit of 120 years, prescribed for man's duration in Genesis 6:3, is subject to considerable variation.

No one knows how long man should live. Science has never dared to set bounds on the possible longevity of man. The reason is that all information as to man's duration is that only which has been, and by no means that which should be.

If a man dies at 75, we may think he has lived long. That thought is based on experience. If one dies at 110, we are amazed by such longevity. If another lives 150 years we are astonished.

Science shows that man's body is constantly being renewed and is apparently intended to go on forever.

When we consider the long preparation that must have been required and was made for the advent of man on earth, it is clear that he was constructed and constituted to live a great many more years than he now lives.

Of all kinds of animal life, man is much the slowest in reaching maturity. He is the only creature that has a prolonged infancy and childhood.

Compare a human baby of one year with a dog, cow or horse of that age. Man reaches complete maturity in about 27 to 30 years, while the cow reaches that stage in about one-seventh of that time. A horse is a complete adult in four years and reaches the age of 40. If that rule be applied to man, he should live 250 to 300 years.

Regardless of what experience shows, advanced physiologists declare that man was not brought into being for the few short and suffering years as he knows today.

Man has always searched for the fabled "Fountain of Youth" but it seems never to have occurred to him to search for it within himself. He has consistently believed that his earthly existence could be prolonged if he knew how to do it.

Ripley, in his "Believe It or Not" of August 3rd, 1937, reported the case of Yekup Shous who was then "157 years old and still going strong" said Ripley, and he added:

"The excellent climate of Abkazia, soviet autonomous republic, a part of Soviet Georgia, Trans-Caucasus, is conductive to long life, and many people there are well over a hundred.

"The oldest of all is Yekup Shous, now 157, and still sprightly and active. Supporting himself on a small cane, he takes daily walks in the mountains, going two miles from his native village, Gveda. His vision and hearing are good, and his memory is so keen that he recalls incidents that occurred about 1800 as though they had happened only yesterday."

WHY DO WE AGE

This region is in the southern part of Russia's part of Asia, on the eastern bank of the Black Sea, and near the site of ancient Babylon, which has a subtropical climate, where once there flourished a great civilization.

A climate favorable to man is one that promotes health and prolongs life. It is not a hostile climate that kills people with extremes of heat and cold, and weakens all those it fails to kill.

In the press of December 27th 1933, we read: "Devastating cold and terrific winter gales and blizzard took a toll of 155 lives as subzero cold spread over the nation in the wake of widespread storms."

The press of January 23rd 1944, said: "Everywhere in the nation, deaths and damages mounted as the cold wave spread." Two days later, the press said: "More than 170 are dead in the wake of storms and zero winds."

In the 1936 heat wave in the same region where people suffered and died of cold, more than 5,000 died of the heat in less than a month.

The press of July 13th, 1936, said: "Michigan sweltered in a heat wave more prolonged than any in its history, and counted 390 deaths in one day attributed directly or indirectly to the six-day siege of 100 degree weather. In the Detroit area 108 deaths were reported in a 14-hour period.

The fact that man attempts to live in such a hostile environment is more evidence of a lack of the basic intelligence of the monkey family, which never of its own accord ventures out of the tropics and subtropics.

Health teachers talk about the Natural Life, and show that such course only can lead to health and longevity. But they appear not to know that man cannot live "The Natural Life" in the land of ice and snow.

In "The Science of Life," Wells and Huxley discuss Old Age under the heading, "The Wearing Out of the Machine," They believe the body wears out and in part wrote:

"The chemical basis of this wearing out is not understood at present. Old age seems to be associated in some way with defective, calcium metabolism. The brittleness of senescent bones is due to the reabsorption of lime salts into the blood. Moreover, there seems to be an accumulation of poisonous substances in the blood.... Sooner or later one or the other of the essential organs fails and the body dies.

"It is more important to realize that our cells do not die because mortality is inherent in their internal structure. They die because they are parts of a very complicated system based on co-operation, and sooner or later one of the tissues lets the others down.

"As a matter of fact, living matter is potentially immoral. If one keeps a culture from the tissues of a young animal and takes sub-cultures regularly, the race of cells can apparently go on growing and dividing indefinitely.

"Death is a consequence of incomplete organization. The tissues die because they are parts of an imperfectly balanced body.

"How long it may be possible for the body to sustain its balance and continue indefinitely, or at least for a much longer period than the common life of the species; is an interesting matter for speculation."

That is the best modern science can do for those who look to it for guidance in matters of health and longevity, and that confirm the statement of Carrel, who said, "In fact, our ignorance (of the body's constitution and function) is profound." (Man, The Unknown. P. 4)

"The tissues die because they are parts of an imperfectly balanced body," assert Wells and Huxley. Be it so, but that condition is the fault of man and not of his body.

The Power to establish and the Mechanism to maintain perfect balance in all departments of the body, is inherent in the organism as a whole and in every organ, gland and cell thereof. No aid from doctors is needed, and no imperfect balance would occur if man lived within the law of his being.

The body needs only to be permitted to operate unhampered in a friendly environment in order to preserve its integrity and equilibrium. The vital process of repair and renewal is automatic in action and perfect in performance; and experiments have shown that the body cells are capable of continuing their work indefinitely unless hindered by man's harmful habits and a hostile environment.

The facts uncovered by every investigation abundantly show that civilized man's conventional mode of living is so faulty to his body and his hostile environment so foreign to his being, that he begins to decline as soon as born, and sinks into degeneracy and death when he should be in his prime.

LONGEVITY (B)

The four gospels of the New Testament picture a people burdened with disorders. A sick multitude appears to have followed the gospel Jesus in his travels, hoping to be healed by some magic process (Matthew 12:13).

It seems not to have occurred to these misguided masses that their ailments are the consequences of their own evil habits and their environment, and that they reap just as they sow (Ga. 6:7).

Ages pass and medical art claims to have made great progress, but conditions of health change not. Multitudes of sufferers still hunt for health, and "medical science" is frantically searching for remedies and cures to the four corners of the earth. Nothing is ever said publicly or officially about the bad habits and a hostile environment.

In the 50-year period from 1332 to 1382 when medical art did not claim to be a "science," a condition called the Black Death and alleged to be an infectious disease, killed 75,000,000 persons in Europe and Asia. That is at the rate of 15,000,000 a year.

What happened 536 years later, after "medical science" had come into being and made great strides in the care of the sick?

In 1918-19 the world was swept by what was termed an influence pandemic, which carried off 21,000,000 victims in less than a year.

Medical art knows no more now than it did a century ago but caring for the sick and preventing sickness. In the same time conditions and habits that ruin health have greatly multiplied. The only factors that hold these in check are better hygienic and sanitary conditions, and not anything done by the medical profession.

People generally know that something is wrong. But few know that the problem is approached in the wrong way. Only a small number of advanced physiologists understand that the work is directed by nonsense instead of by intelligence. If the superstition and mystery surrounding so-called disease were replaced with Natural Science, favorable results would spread like magic and the dawn of a world of health would appear.

If we went back to fundamentals and searched for Causes instead of for Cures, we would discover why the quest of remedies is futile and foolish. We would know why such course can never lead to anything but failure.

The Fountain of Youth is built right into the living organism, and the Law of Physiology describes its operation. Dr. J.C. Dalton, Professor of Physiology in the New York College of Physicians and Surgeons, described the Law of Physiology in these words:

"A continuous change goes on in the substance of the organs of the entire body, by which their structures are constantly being decomposed and constantly renewed. Throughout the whole frame, Vital Force is incessantly engaged in taking apart the tissues of which the body is composed, and in building them over again of new, fresh materials, so that the tissues of the body are accordingly always renewed and always ready to perform their allotted work."

Dalton recites the operation of the process of Perpetual Youth within the body, and because of this physiological process of constant renewal of the entire body, including the largest bones, man's body is never more than seven years old if he live 200 or 2000 years.

WHY DO WE AGE

Seven years is the longest time allotted by advanced physiologists for the complete renewal of the entire body. It is a knowledge of this renewal process, operating incessantly, that prompts scientists to assert that the body is apparently intended to go on forever.

Health and longevity are the direct result of habits and conditions that promote the operation of the Law of Physiology. One of these conditions is a favorable climate that produces a friendly environment. Such climate does not prevail in the land of ice and snow.

In the New York Times of October 28th 1937, appeared an account of an important test made to determine how the body acts in "cold, warm, and comfort zones."

The test was made by Eugene F. DuBois, Professor of Medicine at Cornell University Medical College, and Dr. James D. Hardy, research fellow of the Russel Sage Institute of Pathology. This test showed that:

1. The comfort zone for the human body is between 83 and 90 degrees.

2. In the comfort zone the Mind is at rest, for it is not troubled by the necessity of any function in connection with temperature relation.

3. The body is equipped with the power of perspiration to remove excess heat, and thus protect itself in the warm zone.

4. The body possesses no mechanism to prevent the drain of its vital heat in the cold zone. Its only protection is the exercise produced by involuntary act of shivering.

5. The constant drain of the body's vital heat in the cold zone gradually weakens the body, saps its vitality and shortens its duration.

6. The body is made for the warm zone. It is covered with a thin, delicate skin, is destitute of fur or feathers, is devoid of protection against the cold, and is far better equipped to protect itself in the warm zone than in the cold zone.

The facts disclosed by this test gave valuable information as to the region of the earth in which man is made to live, and the effect of climate and temperature on the body. Yet these paramount factors affecting man's body and life have received in the past but little attention in connection with matters of health and longevity.

It is only in more recent years that advanced students have at last come to realize that Man is made to live in tropical regions that are free of great and sudden changes in temperature from extremes of heat and cold.

WHY DO WE AGE

Under all atmospheric conditions, the body must constantly maintain a steady temperature of approximately 98 degrees, Fahrenheit, to keep in health. Slight variations in body temperature, either up or down, are dangerous.

It is easy for the body to maintain its even temperature when that of the immediate environment is somewhere between 60 and 80. But it is quite difficult when the atmospheric temperature sinks to the freezing point, or to zero or below, and then rises in summer to 105, 110, or 115 in the shade. Under these extremes the vital organs of the body are strained by the extra work required to maintain its even, healthful temperature.

The only region on earth where a perfect climate can be found is in the tropics. There the temperature is regulated by altitude, and one may have the warm weather that prevails in the lowest regions, or the cool weather of the higher regions.

For instance, San Jose, Costa Rica, with an elevation of 3900 feet, has a temperature range from 56 as the coolest part of the night, to 80 as the warmest part of the day.

Costa Rica has three climatic zones – tropical, temperate and cold. These succeed one another as the altitude increases. The tropical zone comprises the coast and the foot-hills, and ranges, in mean annual temperature from 72 to 82 fahrenheit.

In the San Jose plateau, altitude 3000 – 5000 feet, the average is 68 fahrenheit, with an average variation for all

97

seasons of only five degrees. Above 7500 feet frosts are frequent, but snow rarely falls.

The foregoing is true of all tropical regions. Havana, Cuba, has a temperature range of 58 to 88 fahrenheit. The mean winter temperature of Miami, Florida is 68; mean spring, 74; mean summer, 81; and mean fall, 77; mean average, 75 degrees fahrenheit. The variation between the two extremes is only 13 degrees. Such an even temperature is healthful.

Why do most people fade so fast after 40? Why do we dread more and more the approach of cold weather as we grow older? Why does the cold affect us more after 40 than it did when we were 20?

By instinct we dread the cold as we grow older, but force our self to endure it.

If a doctor tells you that a cold climate is not enervating and weakening, he has much to learn. That is true of most doctors.

The enervation effects the whole body, down to every organ and gland. As they begin to fail in function, you whip them up with tonics and stimulants under the doctor's orders. That is the orthodox method of hurting yourself to the grave.

After 40 years of cold weather have left their enervating mark on your body, it is logical that the cold should affect you more than it did when you were only 20 and much more vigorous.

It requires about forty years in most cases for the effect of the slow decline from the work of the cold to become painfully noticeable.

After that, if man still continues in a cold climate, if he still continues to violate God's Plan of Human Life, his decline is usually swift and sure, in spite of tonics and stimulants, and in a few years more he goes to the grave while his friends weep.

Climate makes environment and environment plus his habits make man what he is in the matter of health.

LONGEVITY (C)

"For in the day that thou eatest thereof (consume the body's vital essence) thou shalt surely die" (Gen. 2:7).

In the whole living world there appears strong evidence to show that propagation weakens and destroys, while longevity is gained by non-production.

It may be accepted as an axiom in vegetal physiology that no plant dies a natural death until it has produced and ripened its seed.

If the plant's life is endangered by penury of food or by mutilation, the entire vital force of the plant is concentrated on the production of a flower. It ceases to put forth leaves and expends its whole force in efforts to produce progeny.

This is strikingly exemplified in hot, dry gardens, and by summer waysides, where plants ordinarily of considerable stature, as though conscious of the impending danger, begin to propagate when hardly an inch high.

Plants may have their lives prolonged by nipping off the buds and thus prevent flowering and seeding.

The results of one of the arts of culture makes it seem that there is no such law as a fixed lease of life in plants. The art of propagating by slips and cuttings which, when detached and placed in the soil, will grow into counterparts of the original, and they in turn are extensible after the same manner, affecting for the plant a kind of eternality.

Vines in the days of the Roman Empire have thus been transmitted to the present day, gifted by the work of man, as it were, with a longevity unknown in the natural state.

This would appear as a sort of Fountain of Youth in the case of plants and in the case of man that Fountain of Youth is built right into the body – as we saw by the explanation of Dalton, who showed that –

Every moment of an animal's life witnesses a new receiving, approaching, and giving back – a condition of Senescence and Rejuvenation revolving constantly round each other; dissolution disintegrating over and over again the cells and tissues of the animal, and Creation rebuilding them again new and fresh.

This phase of the law of Physiology constrains leading scientists to assert that the human body, as a machine, is perfect, containing within itself no marks by which they can possibly predict its demise, and apparently intended to go on forever.

It does not appear logical that God should bestow upon plants the power of perpetuity and withhold from man so great a blessing. If it is possible, as experience proves, to prolong indefinitely the existence of plants, then we cannot be wrong in the presumption that the Fountain of Youth is actually in and a part of the living organism, and that the condition which thwarts its legitimate work is the unlawful conduct of man.

For instance, experiments reveal physiological facts that medical art entirely ignores. Elimination is much more important than feeding, but medical art refuses to recognize that fact.

The maintenance of the vital condition of the body is more closely and immediately related to and dependent upon the excreting part of the physiological process than it is upon the supply of new ailment.

Tests conclusively show that feeding may be suspended for a considerable period without causing anything more serious than loss of weight and strength. The records show that people have gone without food all the way from 40 days to 40 years, and still lived and remained in good health.

But the elimination of the effects substances produced by the tissues disintegration cannot be checked for even a few minutes, in warm-blooded animals, without inducing fetal results.

Every act of respiration is in effect the leading process of excretion; for to stay the breathing is to stop the living.

It appears from an ancient legend that in remote times men knew how to live in harmony with the law of their being and reached remarkable ages, some of them living 5,000 years. "The Calmucks had a tradition that men in the first age of the earth lived 80,000 years." Certain secret Thibetan scriptures tell a similar story.

The same law that obtains in the mechanics of inanimate matter appears to operate in the living organism, viz., that which is gained in speed is lost in duration. Intensive action cannot be extensive.

The factor of greater or lesser vital activity is intimately connected with longevity. In proportion to the rapidity of the conduct of the animal in its daily life is invariably the brevity of its duration.
The active conduct which accelerates the vital processes in short-lived animals and brings the lease of life to an early close, is not found in the tortoise and alligator. These latter animals have no sensitive nerve system to quicken the processes of the organism. They spend the greater part of their time in comparative inactivity and, barring accidents, live many centuries.

Of two animals alike in bulk, that one will have the shortest duration which lives the fastest, and that one the longest which lives the slowest.

Annuals which flower when only a few weeks old, die in a few months. Plants live long that bloom not until their fifth or sixth year. The longest ages invariably pertain to those that are the slowest to celebrate their nuptials. It is because trees live so slowly that they live so long, and because animals live so fast that they die so soon.

All the longeval animals live slowly; all the short-lived animals live swiftly. The longeval creatures lead calm, placid lives, as the elephant, swan, tortoise, alligator; while the short-lived ones are no less remarkable for their sportive restlessness, as they course over the hills or sail through the air. Creatures that run or fly much rarely live long.

Conditions of life that bear intimate relation to its duration appear to be connected with generation.

Early puberty forebodes early death. For early puberty shows that maturity will soon be reached and, to learn what happens we hardly need the proverb, "That which is quickly formed, quickly perishes."

The long life span of man, comparatively speaking, follows as a natural sequence of his protracted infancy. Other animals of his size begin to generate and propagate after a much earlier anniversary of birth than he does. They attain their puberty in a few years; some in a few months.

Some exceptions to this rule appear. There is the much quoted instance of the Pike, stated by Bessner to have been captured in 1230 A.D. and to have lived for 267 years afterwards in a Swiss Aquarium. This fish was mentioned in the press of July 24th, 1936, by Ripley in his "Believe It Or Not." Carps are regarded as equally long lived.

WHY DO WE AGE

A certain tortoise lived for 80 years in the garden of the Governor of Cape Town, and is believed to have reached the age of 200 years. Another tortoise, a native of the Galapagos Islands, is known to be 175 years old.

It appears that the antediluvian patriarchs lived nearly a thousand years according to the Bible. No one is competent to declare that these men should then not have lived longer than they did. It would be unwise to hold that the 969 years which Methuselah lived is the extreme limit of man's duration.

It is logical inference that the long duration of life in so-called cold-blooded animals is associated with the slowness of the physiological processes and their conduct of living within the law. The circulation is so slow that the heart of a tortoise beats only 20 to 25 times a minute, and there is no reason to believe that these animals have ever migrated from their natural environment.

Weismann has suggested that one of the factors influencing the duration of life is the fastness or slowness of the vital activities, as above mentioned. This rule fails under examination. Birds are not "cold-blooded" and their vital activities are rapid; yet many of them attain what is considered great ages.

In the Royal Park at Schonbrunn, new Vienna, a white-headed vulture lived to be 118 years old, a golden eagle 104, and a falcon 162. It is logic al to assume that in their wild state these fowls had lived much longer.

H. Milne-Edwards, many years ago, contended that there is no importance in the supposed law of relation between gestation and longevity. He sums up his criticism as follows:

"Although the period of uterine life is longer in the horse than in man, the horse has a life-span shorter than man's and some birds, the incubation of which lasts only a few weeks, live more than a century."

The incubation period of domestic geese is 30 days, and their period of growth is short. But they reach great ages, cases of 80 or 100 years being on record. The gestation period of the horse is longer than that of man. It is a complete adult in four years and it dies of old age at 40.

It appears to be a law that in animals of limited fecundity the duration of life is longer. Eagles and vultures nest only once a year, and generally rear two or often only one nestling, and they live 100 years.

Animals that produce prolifically generally have a relatively brief duration of life. Mice, rats, rabbits and other rodents produce with enormous rapidity, and seldom live more than five or ten years. In view of this, E. Metchnikoff observed:

WHY DO WE AGE

"It is almost possible to imagine that there is some sort of intimate link, possibly physiological, between longevity and low fertility." – Prolongation of Life, P. 44.

After discussing various theories as to the cause of the duration of life, Mr. Oustalet reached the conclusion that food is an important factor. He held that there is a "definite relation between diet and longevity. For the most part, herbivorous animals live longer than carnivores ones" – (La Nature, P. 378).

Simplicity of living also enters the picture. Researchers have found that most centenarians have been poor people, of humble circumstances, who have thus been forced to lead a simple life... existing on a frugal fare.

Centenarians among the rich and opulent are extremely rare, and when found it is also discovered that they also lived a simple life.

Poverty means sobriety and frugality, and there is overwhelming evidence to show that simplicity of living promotes health and prolongs life. It would be the opposite if medical art were right in its claim that feasting on good food produces good health.

The biblical record of the ancient patriarchs supports the theory that an intimate relation prevails between protracted infancy, prolonged puberty and propagation.

When these men did not begin to produce offspring until they were 100 years old, they lived nearly a thousand years; whereas they lived less than two centuries when they began to breed at the early ages of 30 and 35.

Methuselah begat his first offspring when he was 187 years old and died at 969. Nahor first became a father at the age of 29 and died at 148.

The evidence shows that the Law of Generation and the Law of Longevity are reciprocal and compensatory in action, ruling with practically equal force and certainty in both the vegetal and animal kingdoms.

In modern cities, filled with adverse elements and influences that ruin health and shorten life, man matures rapidly, at the expense of more, complete development, and the Generative Function grows acute, abnormal, making man the victim of carnal lust and nocturnal emissions. The latter is an involuntary loss of vital Essence that weakens the body and shortens life.

This is the Law of Generation... in intensive action, in fulfillment of the law of Perpetuity. For if the weakened individual is to perpetuate himself in compliance with the law, it must be done quickly before he sinks into an early grave; as the adverse factors of his environment and his evil mode of living are rapidly destroying him.

As the Generative Function becomes acute, the victim yields to the lust of the flesh and freely indulges to his ruin, in the sacred act that duplicates creative work, and should never be performed except in compliance with the law of Propagation.

The Law of Generation, intensified in action, increases the process of the Law of Degeneration. For every act of coition and every loss of the Vital Essence, whether voluntary or involuntary, weakens the body and drags the victim nearer to the grave – just as the flower diets after it has served its appointed purpose by producing and ripening its seed.

THERE IS NO DISEASE

In 1932 a certain doctor wrote: "The National Conference on Nomenclature of Disease will shortly issue a book for physicians which will rename all known diseases and is expected to include between 10,000 and 20,000 titles in its 250 pages.

"If this were not so serious it would be funny; and that is no joke, for there is but one disease, and giving it 19,999 different names will not teach anybody that his health depends on what goes into his mind, what goes down his neck in the way of food and drink, and the amount of rest, work, fresh air and sunshine he receives."

In 1924 Dr. G. R. Clements wrote a booklet entitled UNITY AND SIMPLICITY OF DISEASE in which he showed that there is but one disease -- bad health. (Now incorporated into the book, The History of Natural Hygiene, from Health Research).

In 1925 he wrote a work titled LAW OF DISEASE AND CURE in which he quoted twelve leading doctors, who have lived and written on human ailments in the last century, showing that-

"Disease is a warning. It is a friend, not a foe. It manifests itself in various forms, from a slight cold to the most severe inflammation, such, for instance, as pneumonia, for the sole purpose of ridding the body of accumulated poisons," -- Dr. George S. Weger

"To cure disease, to restore a lost function of the body, is a natural, physiological process inherent within the body itself. There is no other known agent nor means that can be substituted for it." -- Dr. Albert C. Geyser.

Another doctor, of years of experience and of wide reputation, wrote: "So-called disease is an imaginary entity that does not exist. There are two conditions of the body. (1) good health and (2) bad health. The symptoms of bad health the doctors are trained to study, group together, and give them names (diagnosis) which mean nothing, and term them diseases that will kill the patient if not treated and "cured."

"That scheme of medical art is supported by centuries of false teaching, by which the doctors have been able to create a false psychology of disease that yields gigantic profits; and woe unto him who interferes with that profitable racket."-- Health Science.

WHY DO WE AGE

Dr. Alexis Carrel, then on the medical staff of the great Rockefeller Institute, in an address at the annual meeting of the trustees of Mt. Sinia Hospital on March 22, 1925, said:

"Disease of all kinds are, and have been for centuries, steadily increasing, and humanity has more prospects now, than ever before, of being tortured by some form of cancer, afflicted with slow disease of the kidneys, the circulatory apparatus, the endocrine glands, of becoming insane, of suffering from nervous disease.

"The insufficiency of medicine is embarrassingly flagrant when it deals with tumors.

"What are the determining factors of Cancer? What is its nature? What are the causes of rendering the human organism susceptible to malignant tumors?

"No one today can give a scientific answer to these questions. We do not know what produces arterial hypertension.

"Our ignorance of the cause of chronic diseases and of most of the diseases of the circulatory system is practically complete. Our lack of knowledge is still greater in the nervous and chiefly in the mental diseases, the nature of which remains almost as mysterious as it was during the Middle Ages."

111

That frank acknowledgement by a great physician of the state and condition of medical art creates a far different picture than most of those carried in the big periodicals and publications controlled by the medical and drug trust. It is a picture which medical art tries to keep concealed in the "medical closet."

That state of "the insufficiency of medicine" as Dr. Carrel termed it is the basic reason why the drugless professions were born and why they are growing so rapidly.

Congressman E. Y. Berry, of South Dakota, on June 19, 1956, in the House of Representatives in Washington, D. C., made a speech titled "Health Service is a Basic Right of All the People," in which he said that: --
"In its sixty-year history, Chiropractic has grown to become the second largest branch of the healing arts (in this country), with over 25,000 doctors now licensed to practice this important healing profession."

Regarding the amazing growth of Chiropractic, Dewey Anderson, Doctor of Philosophy, director of the Public Affairs Institute, Washington, D. C., said:

"From a handful of patients somewhat more than half a century ago who came to D. D. Palmer (discoverer of chiropractic) and got relief, those being cared for today by Chiropractors number many millions. And every year the number swells... as their satisfied and healthy patients spread the word. Here is the best and final test of an emerging profession that is seriously serving the public."

We must remember that it is "the flagrant insufficiency of medicine" that drives the sick and suffering into the hands of the Chiropractor, and that it is the efficient and effective work of the Chiropractors that has caused the startling growth of Chiropractic in little more than half a century from one Chiropractor with "a handful of patients" to a growing profession of more than 25,000 licensed doctors of Chiropractic with millions of "satisfied and healthy patients (to) spread the word" of the wonderful work being done by these Doctors of Chiropractic.

We want to mention in particular the work of one Chiropractor who read the work by Clements titled "Unity and Simplicity of Disease."

This particular Chiropractor operated a sanitarium and decided to make a test to see whether all ailments would respond favorably to the same mode of care, which was outlined as follows:
1. The Breath of Life comes first. When we stop breathing we stop living. To preserve life, the air must be free of pollution. Accordingly, patients should be put where they may breathe only fresh, clean, outside air.
2. The Fluid of Life comes next. Man can't live long without water. The greater part of the blood and body consists of water. To preserve life, the water one drinks must be pure and free of the pollutions used by the

political health boards, and also free of solids held in solution, as in the case of water from wells, springs, lakes, and rivers. Accordingly, patients should be given only pure rain water.

3. The greatest Freedom of Vital Function comes next. This is produced by physiological rest of the body's organs, secured only by an absolute fast, giving patients no food but air and water, the two greatest of all foods.

Under this simple, natural regime, his patients recovered as though by magic, regardless of the name that the doctors had given to their ailments.

This Chiropractor was so amazed and so pleased with the results, that he continued it for ten years, taking all patients that came to him and giving them all the same kind of care. Most of the patients were cases which failed to respond to the best medical treatment and were given up as incurable physical wrecks. They all got well; he never lost a patient.

One of these patients was a victim of arthritis in knees and ankles and had been in a wheel-chair for four years. She had failed to respond to the best medical treatment. In five days she was able to walk with no pain in her legs.

Another was a victim of tuberculosis, a man of 29, treated for three years by medical doctors without results. He came prepared to stay six weeks, and went home in three.

Another man of 72 with enlargement of the prostate gland, for which the medical doctors had nothing to offer but an operation, went home well in five weeks.

Another was a veteran of World War 1, who had been thru the regular "immunizing processes" to which all soldiers must submit. He was fit when drafted, but made so unfit by the "immunizing processes" that he was discharged as not fit for service.

He developed a bad case of shaking palsy (paralysis agitans). His hands were so shaky that he was unable to write. Within ten days he was delighted to find his hand had grown so steady that he could write a letter, something he had been unable to do for seven years.

We could go on and on and cite case after case, none of which had responded to medical treatment, and of many and various kinds, that had rapidly recovered under the natural, scientific method outlined above.

We could tell the story of another prominent doctor, who has been doing this same thing for thirty years, -- all of which proves by test and experience that what medical art calls "disease" is nothing more than the symptoms of bad health.

How to rid ourselves of bad health? Not by putting into the body poisons called "medicine". There is no such thing as "medicine."

We get rid of bad health by building good health, not by treating the symptoms of bad health. And we build good health in the sick body by following the natural, simple, scientific regime described above.

If we never violated the rules of health, nor submitted to the health destroying process of "immunization" as advocated and practiced by medical doctors, we would never be sick.
But children cannot go to school in most states in this country now, without being "immunized" against disease" by having the poisonous serums and vaccines of medical art injected into their healthy bodies.

The general public does not understand the rationale of the action of "immunizing agents". They weaken the body by dulling the nerve system and that prevents the body from reacting "acutely" to the damaging internal poisons.

As the body is now too weak to throw off these poisons in the action called "acute diseases", they remain in the body and corrode the internal organs and develop into dangerous chronic disorders.

So, instead of Johnny's having measles when he was six or seven years old, and thus eliminating the damaging internal poisons, they remain in the body and he dies of cancer when he is 35 or 40.

Then medical art rakes in millions annually with its sly slogan, "Fight Cancer with your dollars."

GREAT EPIDEMICS

In the press of March 1, 1948, under a Washington dateline, appeared a news item headed "U.S. Guards against Plague that killed 25,000,000 in Europe." The article says:

"Six Hundred years ago, in 1348, the black death swept Europe. It was one of the greatest calamities of all time.

"Millions died, and historians estimate that by the end of the century the disease had killed up to one-fourth of Europe's population, or possibly 25,000,000 persons."

An analysis of the facts show that in the 50 year period from the year 1332 to 1382, when medical art did not claim to be a "science"; a condition called Black Death, and alleged to be an infectious disease, killed 75,000,000 a year.

Now consider what happened some 536 years later, "medical science" had been born and had "discovered how to conquer disease."

In the winter of 1918-19 the world was swept by what was termed the influenza pandemic, which sent to the grave 21,000,000 victims in less than one year.

And yet medical art points with pride to its progress, and claims to be conquering disease.

As medical art continues its blood-poisoning work of vaccination and inoculation to "conquer disease, "it will not be surprising to see a condition arise some day that will sweep 50,000,000 victims to the grave in one year.

A certain publisher has issued a circular with this sub-headings: "Where have the greatest strides of Medical Science taken us?" and then continues:

"After a glance at the medical records covering the past seventy years of what is boastingly called our great strides in medical science, we can hardly help wondering whether those seven league strides haven't been in reverse, for there has been a marked decrease in our nation's health and a shocking increase in many diseases, which have only been masked and re-named "to save face."

"The acute diseases that were supposed to have been conquered by vaccination, were merely suppressed because the body was so seriously weakened that it was unable to eliminate the internal poisons; and these poisons, aided by the poisonous vaccines, remained in the body, corroded the vital organs, and developed into dangerous chronic diseases.

"The following table reveals facts to show what medical art is doing to the people:

"Increase in Killer Diseases during the past 70 years.
        "Insanity increased   400%
        "Cancer increased   308%

"Anemia increased   300%
"Epilepsy increased   397%
"Bright's Disease increased   65%
"Heart Disease increased   179%
"Diabetes increased   1800% (in spite
of or because of insulin)
"Polio increased   680%

"Although there are a number of far more successful and efficient systems of caring for the sick in this country, the medical system is the only one that gets the endorsement and support of the government.

"All our tax supported Departments of Health, hospitals, and institutions are under the domination of medical personnel.

"In spite of the public financial support, public confidence and full scale experimentation and testing of all their methods and theories, the orthodox medical school has utterly failed to control (or decrease) any of the killer diseases, and does not have a cure for even one of the mild diseases.

"Smallpox and other epidemics were largely controlled by improvements in sanitation and nutrition years before vaccination became popular."

HEART DISEASE

As there is no disease, there can be no heart disease. Yet people are dropping dead all over the nation of what doctor's term "heat disease."

Naturists and hygienists have shown that polluted air paralyzes the breathing control centers of the brain, and breathing stops. That is the end. You are gone. Doctors call it heart disease. They are wrong again.

More light is thrown on the subject by comparing country and city death-rates of this so-called heart disease.

In rural regions where the air is less polluted, the death-rate from so-called heart diseases is given by investigators as 243.6 persons per 100,000 population, while in large cities it is 353.5 persons per 100,000 population -- nearly 40% more than in the country.

In small towns of 2,500 to 10,000 population, it is 317.7. In medium sized cities, 10,000 to 100,000, it is 321.8 persons per 100,000 population.

And as usual, the dumb doctors are unable to account for the steady increase in the death-rate from the better air of the country to the bad air of the larger cities. It is a mystery to them. They lay it to the work and worry incident to city life.

You see the basic causes of sickness must be kept hidden, shrouded in mystery which calls for more dollars for more "research". For the very day that this medical mystery of disease is solved, uncovered, revealed, then and there comes to an end the sweetest racket on earth.

www.ingramcontent.com/pod-product-compliance
Lightning Source LLC
Chambersburg PA
CBHW050215270326
41914CB00003BA/426